CIVILIANIZED

REPLY TO
ATTENTION OF

CIVILIANIZED

1.

confined in our memorandum

early does not apply to
(applicable only to military and civilian

A YOUNG VETERAN'S MEMOIR

—— BY MICHAEL ANTHONY ——

4.

movement, weapon capabilities   enemy strength.

5.   are responsible
Accordingly, they are highly trained and
cultural and socio-
economic backgrounds.

PULP.

Everything that follows is true based on Michael's memory and journal entries of this time period; however, names for several of the people appearing in here have been changed, as well as small details to protect their identities.

PULP. AN IMPRINT OF ZEST BOOKS

2443 Fillmore Street, Suite 340, San Francisco, CA 94115 | www.zestbooks.net
Connect with Zest! zestbooks.net/blog | twitter.com/zestbooks | facebook.com/BooksWithATwist

Manufactured in the U.S.A. | 4500629222 | DOC 10 9 8 7 6 5 4 3 2 1

1

I was visiting my brother Keith in San Diego, and we were getting drunk at some crappy rundown sports bar. It was your typical hole in the wall that attracted parole violators, dingy prostitutes, and college kids. Paint was peeling off the walls. Someone was puking in the bathroom, and even though smoking indoors was outlawed, everyone was doing it anyway. I'd been in bars like this before: the lights were dimmed to keep people from noticing the roaches, and the heat was turned off so people would drink to stay warm. In this case, only the latter worked.

Mingling with the bugs and rodents in full view, men and women were dressed in outrageous Halloween costumes. There were nurses, vampires, police officers, gladiators, aliens, and even a Jesus. In the corner of the room, at a wobbly, broken-down table, I stood with my brother, just watching. It wasn't the crowd you'd expect to be excited about Halloween, but the bar offered a cash prize, so everyone was into it.

The costumes were interesting, and the girls cute, but my mind was someplace else.

Two weeks earlier, I'd returned home after twelve months in Iraq. I was addicted to sleeping pills and painkillers, I was drinking and smoking too much, and it'd been two years since I'd even kissed a woman.

"Here's what I think," Keith was saying, after chugging the rest of his beer. "Being in the army is like having sex, but with someone you hate—"

I laughed.

"It's not great, but it's still sex, so how bad can it really be?"

It didn't seem quite that simple to me, though. I'd always heard that the hardest part about returning from war—

"I'll be right back," Keith staggered from the table. "Tell the waitress to bring me another Corona. I'm gonna change into my costume—"

The hardest part is adjusting to the changes that happen while you're away.

"—the competition's about to start."

The world goes on without us. Before I went to Iraq, Keith—my second oldest brother and a non-combat army vet—drank Budweiser and lived in Massachusetts. Now that I was back, he drank Corona and lived in California.

"Two Bud Lights," I yelled to the waitress as my brother lurched his way to the bathroom. It was only 10 p.m., and I was already drunk. The real kind, too. The kind where I'd be slamming my fists on the table in a minute. And if I'm being honest, I was also high on Vicodin. In Iraq, everyone had aches and pains, and since Vicodin was the most prescribed painkiller, it was hard to avoid some level of addiction. I had popped two before the bar, and I'd had four shots and six beers; I could barely feel my arms and legs. In fact, there was only one thing I could feel, the only thing on my mind besides drinking and taking pills: anger. An anger that surged and subsided, but never disappeared.

In Iraq, I felt alive. More alive than I ever had before. The rush from constant near-death experiences was like no other. Running for my life toward a cement bunker. Looking Death in the eye and saying, "Not today." It made me *feel*. That intensity, that passion, that adrenaline, I wanted it back—and the only way for me to get even a fraction of that feeling back was to fight. I had to fight someone big, someone ferocious, someone who would make me feel fear at least.

I lit a cigarette and a cloud of smoke dropped into my lungs; it was my fifth in a row, and my stomach twisted as I inhaled. I felt like I hadn't eaten in days, and as I looked around the bar, contemplating whether to order a sandwich—

"Hey. Move it, asshole!" someone yelled.

I whirled around, expecting some preppy college kid dressed as Captain Kirk, but, instead, a massive Hell's Angel stood in front of me. The man was built like an ox, and right away I knew he was legit: the sleeve tattoo, the chain wallet, an enormous Hell's Angel patch on his leather jacket, and three cronies and two girls standing behind him, dressed the same way with the same patches. This was no costume.

The biker slapped his hand on my shoulder. I glanced up at the ceiling. *Thank you*, I silently prayed. It was time to fight.

"Get your fucking hand off me!" I said to the biker, not because I expected him to move his hand, but to expedite the confrontation. I took a quick drag of my cig, puckering my lips like I was going in for a kiss, and blew smoke in his face.

His eyes narrowed. "Listen," he snarled, like an old drill sergeant. "This is our table; so take your shit and leave!" He puffed out his chest, as alpha males have done since the beginning of time, and looked me in the eye. Our faces were inches apart. I stared back and he smiled; it was the quick, effortless smile of a wolf enjoying the hunt. I studied the retinas of his beady eyes. He was either on crack or coke. He leaned forward, and I smelled burnt hot dogs and tequila.

"Let's just leave, Jack," one of the women said.

"Yeah," I turned my back to him and spoke over my shoulder, "Why don't you hit the road, Jack."

Standing at five-foot-nine and one-hundred-fifty pounds, my gangly frame was nothing compared to Jack's. He was masssive. He could've broken me.

Jack said something to his cronies, and then turned around and started leaning backward. He pushed the full weight of his body into me. The studs on his leather jacket dug into my spine while his ponytail tickled my neck. (I'd never been tickled by a biker before.) I pushed back into him with all of my weight, leaning as hard as I could, but he didn't even budge. I had thoughts of giving up and walking away, but those quickly faded as I looked over at one of Jack's pals—three hundred pounds of filth, with a separate beard for each of his four chins—and he was laughing. I looked over at the girls; they were laughing, too.

That's it, I told myself, and chugged the rest of my beer. *No one laughs at me, I'm a goddamn veteran.* I took a final drag of my cig, then moved out from under Jack's weight, grabbed an empty bottle by the neck, and flipped it upside down. I closed my eyes, and I heard my drill sergeant telling me about *first blood*.

"Just let your thoughts disappear," he'd say. "Clear all thoughts and then follow through with pure action."

I turned and focused on the back of Jack's head. Silence rang in my ears. I was ready to fight, to kill even. But before I could raise my arm to bring the bottle down on Jack's head, I saw a pair of pasty, sandal-clad chicken legs sticking out of a bright yellow banana costume. The ghastly banana suit ended just above the knee, and it was easy to tell that my brother Keith was stark naked underneath. My gaze went from Keith to the back of Jack's head.

Music suddenly started playing, or had always been playing, and all at once a thousand different sounds hit my eardrums. I looked down. The empty bottle was apparently less empty than I thought, and the remaining contents had been slowly dripping down my sleeve.

"Hey..."

I glanced at the cigarette in my hand. I thought I had finished it, but I somehow had a new one already lit. "Hey, Jack..." I tried to remember what it was we'd learned in school: *Stop, Drop and Roll*! No, that was for fire emergencies. *Just Say No*? No, that was for drugs and alcohol. I gave up, and flicked the cigarette directly at him.

I grabbed Keith's arm. We ran.

A moment later, we burst through the barroom doors. As soon as the cool ocean air hit my lungs, I lit a new cigarette. I felt good.

2

I looked at the crumpled piece of paper in my hand. I dialed: 1-8-0-0-2-7-3-8-2-5-5. Thirty seconds later, I found myself wondering why the hell a suicide hotline operator would start a conversation by asking how I was feeling. Wasn't it obvious? What did she expect people to say? "Oh, you know, I'm doing all right, I'm just calling to see how *you're* doing."

I told the lady—the operators are almost always ladies—that when I walked around I felt hollow, as if I were a puppet without strings or a disemboweled mummy. I told her I felt like I wasn't there, that I felt like God shoved a vacuum cleaner up my ass and sucked everything out. I told her I'd felt like that since coming home.

"Let's make a list," the lady said. She was trying to sound friendly, yet serious.

"Excuse me?"

"You know. A list. We'll make a list of everything you enjoy."

Keith and I had gotten back from the bar two hours earlier. He was already passed out, the banana costume crumpled on the living room floor. I, on the other hand, had taken a couple of sleeping pills, which—combined with the Vicodin, booze, and nicotine—were starting to make me feel pretty woozy. My body didn't know whether to pass out for the next sixteen hours or to never sleep again. I leaned back on the couch and put my feet up on Keith's coffee table.

"Come on," the operator playfully said. "Let's make a quick list. Besides, what have you got to *lose?*"

I let out an unexpected chuckle.

I didn't know what to tell her. There wasn't much that sprang to mind. But she wouldn't give up, and after several minutes of going back and forth, I came up with something: cigarettes. The truth was, though, that I didn't really feel like talking any longer. I was starting to feel bad.

Two weeks earlier, I had been in Iraq working in a combat support hospital. I assisted doctors during surgery. I cauterized wounds, sutured skin, and sawed through limbs, all while trying to stay alive. Soldiers, terrorist, civilians: they all passed through our doors. We believed that we were helping to make the world a better place. We believed that we were fighting to help our country. But nothing seemed better. No jobs were available, people were rude, politicians lied, and the news covered celebrity gossip more than the wars. I felt like my brothers in arms were dying for no reason and that no one gave a shit.

The funny thing was, I didn't want to think about it either. I didn't want to think about all the civilians and soldiers who died. I didn't want to think about the politics. I'd had enough. It wasn't that I wanted to die; it was just that I didn't want to live. "I miss being overseas, in Iraq," I said as I cleared my throat. "I miss the friendships, the sense of purpose, the adrenaline, the hope." I tried telling her more, but she kept changing the subject.

"Let's focus on things back home," she said. "It might be better to—"

"I guess I still enjoy reading books." It was getting late and I could feel the pills fighting it out in my stomach. "But, I mean, a good book." My stomach rumbled. "It has to be a good one."

"How about writing? Do you like writing?"

I closed my eyes; the sleeping pills were winning the battle. I told her yeah, that I did write, that I was writing a story about my friend Crade. I told her that Crade was the first person I met when I joined the army. He took me under his wing and introduced me to everyone. I told her that he was a great guy and everyone loved him. He even had a baby on the way. I told her that one day in Iraq, out of the blue, he tried to kill himself.

"Did you blame yourself for it?" she asked.

"What? No." I sat up straight. "I mean, he's still alive, it was just an attempt. But what I'm saying is that it's, like, a slap in the face because Crade was a good guy. He had a good life. And what the hell does it mean when someone with a better life than you tries to kill himself? It's a fucking insult, that's what it is… and I… I did actually try to stop him." The drugs were fucking with me; I couldn't keep a train of thought. "If a guy saw a person more depressed than him, at least he could always say, 'Hey, I've got it better than that guy,' but you couldn't say that with Crade. He did try to kill himself… he did actually try, and—"

Beer flew out of my mouth, along with half-digested pills and chunks of something brown (even though I couldn't remember eating anything in days). After a few more dry heaves, the woman on the phone was still talking.

"Are you okay, Mike?" she asked.

I wiped my mouth.

I had no idea when or how it happened. I must have blacked out, but we both suddenly knew each other's names.

"Yeah, I'm okay."

I looked down at my shirt and pants; it looked like a colostomy bag had exploded over me, but at least my stomach didn't hurt as much. I ignored the mess, and Jill and I continued to talk. My list began to grow. Now, along with cigarettes, it included war, fighting, good books, steak, *Seinfeld* reruns, Vicodin, throwing rocks at signs, Ambien, and sex. (Jill insisted that I add sex to the list. "Come on, everyone loves sex," she said, and since I didn't have the heart to tell her that I hadn't been kissed, much less been laid in two years, I let her add it anyway.)

"Why'd you call today?" Jill finally asked.

They asked me that every time I called—twice in the last two weeks. It was kind of a weird question, but I figured they asked it more out of curiosity than anything else. If I had all kinds of people calling me every day and telling me how depressed they were, I guess I'd be curious, too.

"Um, you know, the typical stuff."

"Come on, Mike." She adopted a tone of familiarity, as though we were old friends.

"No, it's nothing." I needed to get off the phone. My head was spinning. I needed water. "I just need to take some time to think. I'm fine."

"Are you sure?" She sounded hesitant.

"The list was a big help."

Jill sounded concerned as she took a deep breath and asked if I was going to do anything that I might regret. I wasn't sure what to tell her. I said again that I was fine. My hands were shaking. I couldn't think straight; goosebumps appeared all over my arms, and the room felt as though it'd dropped twenty degrees. Something was starting to hit me... hard. I needed to sleep. I tried to tell Jill that she was doing a great job and that I'd call back one day when I was feeling better, but most of it just came out as mumbles.

"And just remember," she said, sounding as though she were smiling, "the depression will probably go away sooner rather than later. And I *bet you* that any negative feelings will be gone in three months, max. Leading psychologists say—"

I didn't want to hurt her feelings. I just wanted the feelings to end—hers, mine, everyone's. "Three months..." I paused. It seemed as good a timeframe as any other. "Okay, three months."

"Just *promise me*," she pleaded, "that you won't—"

I looked down at the coffee table. There was a newspaper there, alongside all the spilled beer and vomit. The paper was flipped open to a story about a bombing in Iraq, or Afghanistan, or somewhere. A handful of people had died, possibly American or Iraqi, or Afghan. Whatever, it didn't matter. I looked at the bottle of Vicodin. I looked at the newspaper. There were hundreds of thousands dead from the wars, millions injured, and I didn't care. That was the worst part. While we were over there, we had to turn that part of ourselves off. I hated myself for it, but nothing changed.

I decided that if I wasn't out of this emotional abyss in three months, I was just going to end the emptiness, the quickest way possible.

"How many suicidal people does it take to change a light bulb?"

She didn't answer.

"None. They just—"

"Please... Michael, just think..."

I hung up. [1]

---

1. Since the inception of the Veteran Administration's suicide-prevention hotline in 2007, they've received an average of 50,000 calls a year.

3

The police officer shook his head.

"Are you kidding me?" he kept repeating.

It was two days after my conversation with Jill, and I had just been caught relieving myself in an alley.

"I-I-I-" I stammered.

It was midnight and I was standing next to a flat, barracks-style bar where I'd just spent the last three hours. It was a windowless place, suffused with the acrid smell of cheap beer. A few scraggly haired guys playing pool beneath fluorescent lights completed the scene. It had been my go-to bar for the past few days. I was staying clear of the Hell's Angel bar after the latest incident—and so was Keith. He was stuck at home with his wife. She was pregnant and pissed at me for almost getting him into a fight, which meant that I'd been going solo. This new place was such a shithole that I figured no one would mind if I pissed against the outside wall after this latest smoke break. But this police officer appeared to disagree.

He grabbed the back of my shirt. "Have some self-respect," he said, and pulled me out of the alley. We were back on the sidewalk when he pushed me into a palm tree. I could barely keep upright. "Get the hell out of here!" he yelled.

I mumbled back something to the effect of "Mmhm," and held onto the tree that he'd pushed me into, using it to keep my balance. I steadied myself long enough to light a cigarette.

A bright orange flyer was taped to the tree trunk:

Change Your Life!
Learn to Attract Women!

I took a long drag.

There was a group of good-looking girls on the flyer—all of them sitting with some skinny white guy—along with a phone number and website. I'd seen this thing—or things like it—elsewhere and online, but for whatever reason this was the night that I actually took notice.

The advertisement was for a three-day self-improvement course. It cost two thousand dollars and included daytime sessions that would cover the topics of: Modern Masculinity, Approaching Women, Attracting Women, Sealing the Deal, and finally, Secret Techniques. The nighttime sessions consisted of Practical Application.

Twenty-four hours later, I was sitting on a couch that smelled like mothballs. It was flowered and part of a generic executive suite in a shitty Marriott hotel: white walls, bland carpeting, another couch, and a table in the center of the room. Beside me sat three other men: Bob, a middle-aged computer programmer; Chuck, a private contractor in his thirties; and Jarrod, a skinny kindergarten teacher of indeterminate age. I was the youngest of the group. The four of us were crammed on the couch while a fifth, a freckled, curly haired hippie, stood in front and lectured at us in a Midwestern accent.

The hippie's name was David. He was wearing a Bob Marley T-shirt, skintight pants, and a cross around his neck. He was, unbelievably, both an Irish Catholic and our new dating coach. The four of us seated on the couch were students, and we had each paid thousands of dollars to find ourselves here. In return, David would instruct us on how to attract women.

"This is where we take our lives back," David said, throwing his arms in the air. In the short time that we'd been in his hotel room, he'd done nothing but scream at us and thrash his body around. He couldn't stay fucking still—he was like an ape with ADD. "This is where we become men." He pounded his chest.

After buying nothing but books and cigarettes for the last year, I managed to save fifty thousand dollars from my deployment. Why not spend some of it? I had nothing else to do, but I had a limited amount of time to do it in. Three months. I figured it was like those Dying Parties I'd heard about, where people with terminal diseases decide that, instead of wasting away slowly and painfully, they'd rather die with dignity and on their own terms. So they throw a party. Good food. Good drinks. Good people. Then, toward the end of the night, they go upstairs and take a bottle of pills while the guests either stay and party, or stay and pray. It's their way of going out with a bang. Sometimes, as a last "screw you" to the corporate world, they max out their credit cards and buy everyone gifts.

The idea seemed disgusting, scary, poetic, horrifying, sad, intriguing, and a thousand other things—but it also made a kind of sense. I was still young, and I didn't consider myself depressed. In fact, I figured I was the opposite of depressed. Depressed people felt something, I figured, but—aside from an occasional burst of anger—I felt nothing. I was just a vet who no longer wanted to live in the world that he had fought for. And there's no point in keeping an empty container around.

"Confidence is key! Without confidence, manliness is impossible!" David roared.

He went on to tell us that because our genes had survived this long, we were all the alpha males of the species. The other students nodded at that point, as though they'd suspected it all along and just needed confirmation. David then informed us that we were all born "real" men, but because of the mainstream culture, we had picked up undesirable traits that made us weaker. "We need to rid our bodies of these feminine traits and replace them with ones that are positive, masculine—"

He cast his gaze out over everyone, and then stopped on me. He stared until I eventually lowered my eyes. He then shook his head and turned away from me, telling everyone to partner up for the first exercise. He said we should stare into our partner's eyes for ten minutes, take a quick break, and then do it again. As soon as he finished talking, the three other guys jumped up and started moving around. I raised my hand.

"What the hell's the point of this?"

"There's one in every class." David smiled. "Life, man. Expression, man. It's all through the eyes. As men, we've got to be able to hold eye contact with each other." He attempted to stare deeply into my eyes. "It's incomprehensible how *some* men can't even hold strong eye contact."

Bob laughed. "Sing it brother," he said. "Michael's young; he doesn't know how to take it all in and go with the flow. He'll eventually mature." I was at least ten years younger than everyone in the room, and I seemed to be the only one concerned with getting my money's worth.

I looked at Bob, and was almost overwhelmed with the desire to punch him in the face. From our introductions at the beginning of the session, I knew that he'd attended practically every "how to attract women" seminar in the United States. He said he'd spent close to twenty thousand dollars on the programs. He was sixty pounds overweight, hadn't shaved in a month, hadn't washed his hair in over a year, and yet he somehow believed that his inability to hold eye contact was keeping the ladies away.

"Now, now, boys, let's all love one another," David jumped in. "Michael, you work with Chuck, and Bob, you can partner with Jarrod."

Chuck was easily two hundred pounds overweight, and his labored breathing made it seem like he was moments away from death. I couldn't help but wonder how he felt about paying thousands of dollars just to stare into my eyes.

"Ready," David shouted as he clicked his stopwatch, "begin!"

Chuck and I stared into each other's eyes and, after a long minute, his head started to drop to the left. Ten seconds later, his eyes fluttered. Ten more seconds and his chin sagged to his chest. His head dropped down. He quickly picked it up and then, just as quickly, let it drop again. Five seconds later, his eyes fluttered rapidly. Another five seconds, and he closed his eyes. Chuck was asleep.

I cleared my throat. "Ahem."

Chuck's arms flew into the air. He pulled his shoulders back and opened his eyes. He yawned and grunted like a bear waking from hibernation.

We continued staring, and not a minute went by before Chuck fell asleep again. I cleared my throat and Chuck's eyes fluttered open. We continued this dance several times before he finally had an outburst.

"Goddamn it," he exclaimed, "I can't stare into this guy's eyes without falling asleep." Bob and Jarrod stopped staring at each other and stared at me. David looked over, too. "I guess I can see it." David's stopwatch beeped. "Time's up," he said. This cued Bob and Jarrod to rush over and try to stare into my eyes.

"Get the fuck out of here," I said and waved them away.

After a quick smoke, David informed me that Chuck no longer wanted to be my partner and that I'd be working with Bob instead. I'd never really known the proper amount of eye contact to give another man. I'd always figured that if I stared for too long, I was challenging him to a fight, and if I looked away too soon, I was (to borrow a popular army phrase) his bitch. I realized how this thinking had affected my life and how I'd avoided eye contact with other men in attempts to avoid mistakenly inviting either of the two extremes. I had no idea what it meant that Bob and I had been staring at each other for several minutes, but I was still trying to figure it all out when I noticed Bob's head starting to sag. His chin slumped a few inches and his eyes fluttered and closed. Bob was asleep.

Beep.

"Time's up." David leaped from his chair.

Bob groaned and repeatedly blinked his eyes. "How long was I out for?" he asked.

"Oh, not long," I lied. "Just a second."

Everyone stood and stretched their legs as David looked over his notes for the next exercise. *Kino*, it was called, short for the word "kinesthetic," which meant being able to sense your own body. Here, however, *Kino* meant the art of playfully and sexually touching someone. After the break, David sat on the couch and then patted the cushion next to him, "Have a seat, buddy." I hesitated for a moment, but relented when he explained that I wouldn't have to stare into his eyes. As soon as I sat down, though, he smiled creepily. It was a "welcome to my trap" type of smile, the kind I imagined a serial killer might give a victim-to-be.

David told us that he was going to show us a proper scalp massage. "Do this right," he smiled with that same creepy smile, "and I guarantee that you'll keep them coming back for more."

When David finished his instructions, he immediately put

his right arm around me. He pulled me close and placed the palm of his right hand on the top of my head. He started to bring his fingers up and together, gently caressing my scalp. His thick, cold fingers massaged while the other students jotted down notes. I wasn't sure what to think or do. My head was being stroked by another man while others watched, I was high on Vicodin, and to top it all off, my entire body was starting to tingle. My shoulders inadvertently relaxed. I hated myself for it, but it felt good, and David kept massaging as everyone asked questions. Ten minutes later, there were no more questions and no one was taking notes, but David was still caressing my head. We all noticed this, at the same moment, and there was a silence as we exchanged glances. David finally stopped. I stood up. I didn't know if I should take a shower or have a cigarette.

David stood, too. "Break time," he said, and winked at me.

I went to the nearest window and lit a cig. I wasn't sure, but it seemed that my dating coach might have a crush on me.

I suddenly felt it necessary to verify that I wasn't alone in feeling that David was a little too hands-on. While Bob and Chuck joyously practiced massaging each others' scalps, I walked over to Jarrod. Tall, skinny, and completely bald, Jarrod smelled like patchouli oil, clove cigarettes, and Play-Doh. He'd explained earlier that he was a kindergarten teacher, but he didn't look like any teacher I knew. His fishing vest, cargo pants, and combat boots said that he was ready to spend the weekend hunting, but the mesh shirt under the vest and the fedora on his head said that he was ready to go clubbing. Jarrod was in the other corner of the room, talking to David about the nighttime segment of the course, where we'd go to bars and try our new techniques. When David went to the bathroom, I took the opportunity to talk to Jarrod and hear his thoughts.

"Um… I've got a quick question." I approached Jarrod, pausing, deliberating the most appropriate way to pose my question. "So… um… you don't think David's a little… *you know*…." I pushed. "Don't you think?"

"What! No!" Jarrod's jaw dropped. "I'm not gay!"

"No. No." I put my palms in the air. "Not *you*—" I whispered.

"Oh," he responded in a tense whisper of his own. He looked over his shoulder toward Bob and Chuck. "Wait, who do you mean?"

A silence fell between us and I just shrugged. "Forget it." I left Jarrod and crossed to the other side of the room, away from him, Bob, and Chuck. I didn't know if I was pissed or disappointed. Nothing about this class was what I expected, and I began planning a quiet getaway. I was ready to tell the guys that things were getting a little too weird for me when David emerged from the bathroom and began a long spiel about how he loved women with small breasts. "It's the nipples, man," he said. "The smaller the breast, the sexier the nipple. If you ever date a woman with small, perky breasts, have her rub her nipples all up and down your back." (An oddly specific instruction.) He shuddered as though someone had rubbed an ice cube across his spine. "Ooooh, that feels so good."

As David regaled us with more stories of all the girls he'd slept with, a voice within me began to speak of hope and possibility. Perhaps David *was* the real deal. After several brief anecdotes about his experiences with threesomes, David walked over to the other side of the room to get his manual for the next exercises. In his absence, I rejoined the group and tried to blend in a bit more.

"Who knew that learning to meet women would be so homo-erotic, right?" I grinned as I set up my punchline. "I mean, at the rate we're going, for the next exercise he's probably going to have us practice our kissing—"

Ba-da-bing!

I looked around.

Nothing.

Bob rubbed his beard while Chuck lowered his eyes and stared at the ground. I looked over at Jarrod. He was applying ChapStick. "Who knows," he shrugged. "My lips are too dry anyway."

Everyone started talking again once I left the group. I sat on the couch and started flipping through one of the instruction manuals. My heart stopped as I saw the next chapter. It was titled, "Learning How to Hypnotize Women." The class had suddenly gone from weird to scary. I started reading, and I couldn't believe my eyes. I hoped that the title was a metaphor, but the text that fol-lowed, which included the words "hypnotic," "neurolinguistic," and "programming," informed me that it wasn't. I got up to leave.

"It's gotta be his eyes, they're too big or something." Bob grabbed me by my shirt collar as I walked by. "What is it about those eyes, check them out—"

He was laughing when he said it, but I really hate a stretched collar on a T-shirt—and he was still holding mine.

I may be undersized, but between the army and four older brothers, I knew a thing or two about fighting. I grabbed Bob by his own collar, and even though he outweighed me by a hundred pounds, I easily tossed him to the floor. "Touch me again, and I'll fucking kill you, you creep!"

I felt like I did at the bar. Like I did in Iraq. I had that pins-and-needles feeling when a limb falls asleep and then starts to wake back up. I became aware of every inch of my body, pulsating with a sensation of pure testosterone. I was ready to fight.

"Whooa," David yelled as he jumped over the couch and wrapped his arms around me.

I stared at Bob to let him know that I was serious. I could see fear in his eyes. After I was sure that he'd gotten my message, I told everyone that I was fine and pushed David's hands off. "I'm not going to do anything else," I said. "It's done."

There was silence as David helped Bob to his feet. I ignored Chuck and Jarrod—both of whom were still glaring at me. Bob brushed off his pants and apologized for grabbing my shirt. "I was just foolin' around," he said. I regarded him for a moment as he stood in front of me. My heart was still pounding, but I felt pity for him. Unlike the biker at the bar, Bob was helpless and fragile. It's never satisfying to fight when you know you can win.

4

For the field practice section of the course, we met at an upscale
rooftop club. A shallow pool lay at its center, with bars on both
ends. People weren't actually allowed to swim in the pool, but a
mass of people congregated around it, talking, smoking, and dancing. Most of the women were taking pictures as they danced, while
most of the men seemed to be sizing one another up. There was an
ebb and flow to the crowd that reminded me of dogs at a dog park:
lots of play, but also a little menace. My fellow students and I were
spread throughout the club. David had told us that we had to first
hit on women on our own. Later, we'd each get a chance to work
with him individually and see how *he* "worked his magic."

    I had almost skipped the nighttime program, but David didn't
offer a refund, so I figured I'd might as well go. There was another
reason why I showed up. Not only was I curious to see if David's

techniques actually worked—and maybe even meet a girl or two—but I had somehow started to feel for these guys. It was like in war, how the relationships that are forced upon you (soldiers don't choose who they share a foxhole with) can take on a type of unexpected intimacy. It's the shared experience that brings you together, not whether or not you both like video games or basketball or the same band. Even though my classmates weren't combat vets, I realized that we were all fighting our own wars of loneliness. We were in it together. We paid thousands of dollars, not because we wanted to get laid—or not just for that—but because we didn't want to be alone anymore. We were a helpless, hopeless bunch. And I had nominated myself as protector of this motley crew.

I looked through the pack of dancers and, one by one, found *my* group of guys: Bob was in the corner talking to some girls and doing a magic trick, David was busting a move on the dance floor, and Jarrod was talking to a woman by the pool. Chuck hadn't shown since the break.

"Hey you!" I heard someone shriek as I scanned the crowd. I turned around and saw an enormous white dude running toward Jarrod. He pushed people out of the way as he ran, his face twisted with surprise and fury. He was ready to fight.

"Hey, hey, hey," I shouted as I ran over.

It was too late.

The guy headbutted Jarrod in the face.

I jumped between them, my blood pumping. I'd already had three beers and one and a half Vicodins, and I was feeling pretty good.

The guy who had done the headbutting was wearing an untucked, white button-down shirt, backward baseball cap and dark denim jeans, and had a neatly trimmed goatee. Definitely a jealous boyfriend. "Let's take it easy," I said as I placed my hand on his chest and pushed him backward. I figured if anyone was going to fight tonight, it'd be me, not Jarrod. I reached over to put my other hand on Jarrod's chest and push him back, but he was gone. The head-butter was focused on me now. "You got a problem?" I asked.

I stood and held his gaze—this was a type that I was comfortable with. The fighting kind. I had to bite my cheeks, though, because I felt a smile coming on. I tried to stop myself. I didn't want to feel like I was in some ridiculous movie or something, but I couldn't help it. As this dude stared into my eyes, I imagined him falling asleep, like Chuck and Bob had.

"What's so fucking funny?" he asked—not without cause.

Just like that, my smile disappeared. War memories are like every other kind of memory; you can never tell when they'll hit. They flicker in and out like an old high school crush: Even though time passes, you still find yourself flipping through the mental pictures and wondering what could've been. I felt a sudden pressure in my head, like a migraine, but worse. All I could think of was when Sergeant Doff, back in Iraq, had asked me the same question right before he did something that should've gotten him discharged.

The thought cued my anger. I could feel it shuddering inside me. I hated this guy like I had hated Doff.

An eye for an eye, and a headbutt for a headbutt, I guess I figured. I hit the jealous boyfriend in the chin. If I had planned it out, I would have gone for his nose but since this guy easily had six inches on me, his chin was all I could reach.

He cried out, but didn't have time to say or do anything else before blood trickled from his mouth.

His eyes filled with tears. He looked like he was really hurt. I probably must have been too, but I couldn't feel anything through the Vicodin. I was invincible.

Or at least I thought I was. One of the less excellent things about Vicodin is that it severely affects your reflexes. I was too busy looking at his bloody teeth to realize that he was about to land a fist to my stomach. By the time I realized it, it was too late. He hit me right in the belly button; I still didn't feel any pain, but the body's natural reaction to being punched in the gut is to grab wherever you've been hit and bend over. That's a bad idea during a fight.

A minute later, I opened my eyes.

I was curled up like a baby, lying sideways on the ground. I had no idea how I got there, but it wasn't much of a mystery. I glanced at the crowd gathered around.

When my friend Crade had tried to kill himself in Iraq, Sergeant Doff covered up the attempt. Not because Crade asked him to, but because Doff didn't want the unit to look bad: A soldier's attempted suicide wasn't exactly something to brag about. So, instead of helping Crade, he gave him extra duty as punishment. Two weeks later, Crade tried to kill himself again. Then, as if Doff hadn't given us enough reasons to hate him, he also ordered me to cover guard duty for a woman he was sleeping with at the time (both of them were married to people back in the States). His dereliction of duty and abuse of power knew no bounds, but I never said anything. It was part of the soldier's code of silence.

"Hey!" yelled someone in a tight black shirt and sunglasses. A bouncer, most likely. He stood over me. "What's going on here?"

The shouting from the crowd began instantly. "He deserved it," someone said. "It was his own fault," another voice hollered. A dozen more chimed in: "I saw the whole thing." "I think he might be dead." "Where's the other guy?"

"Get up." The bouncer picked me up.

"Get your *fucking* hands off my collar—"

He slammed me into a wall.

"You pansy ass, piece of—"

He slammed me again.

I couldn't move. My heart was pounding.

"Just get the hell out of here," he finally said, releasing me.

I hadn't expected him to just let me go. I pushed him backward as hard as I could. He barely budged. Then he pulled his left arm back. I knew what was coming, but, again, the Vicodin. This time, as I took an uppercut in the stomach, I could actually hear the wind rush out of me. *At least I'm still conscious*, I thought.

Then I wasn't.

5

Bob, Jarrod, David, and I walked together along the clean streets of San Diego. After getting kicked out of the first club, we started walking past one street and the next and the next. Overall, I was feeling pretty good—my nose aside.

I couldn't remember how Bob, Jarrod, and David had wound up leaving with me, but I remembered holding a blood-soaked napkin to my nose as we walked out. At one point during our prowl, I stopped in at a convenience store and bought another pack of cigarettes. I asked if anyone else needed anything beforehand, but nobody answered. They were all giving me the silent treatment, probably for something that Jarrod had told them about the fight. But that was just fucking fine by me.

The smell of cigarettes and cheap cologne permeated the walls of the next club, which also happened to be on a rooftop, and which featured a collection of bouncers that seemed much less intimidating. David and I both headed for the bar while Jarrod and Bob hit the dance floor.

"I've got a line for you," David whispered into my ear. He'd been whispering in my ear ever since we got to the new club, like he was a spy or something. It didn't exactly make me feel comfortable, but after everything that had happened during his class earlier, it was the least intimate exchange between us. "Walk up to that girl in the skimpy black dress and tell her that she has the sexiest calves in this entire club."

I coughed and almost spit out my beer.

"Trust me," he said. "Just use what I taught you."

I took a deep breath and silently mulled over his pick-up line.

In high school, I was never able to talk to girls. I was introverted, to say the least: a JD-Salinger-reading, journal-keeping nerd. I was able to endlessly rehash old *Seinfeld* jokes, but girls weren't always impressed with that particular skill. Friends of mine would even tell girls to talk about their bra sizes and sex lives in front of me, just to see me blush. I was weird and I was awkward ("wicked weird," "wicked awkward," as they said in Massachusetts), and everybody knew it. *But screw it*, I thought. I wasn't in Massachusetts anymore, and this wasn't high school.

I'd spent twelve months in a war zone, been in thirteen mass-casualty situations, helped deliver ten babies, participated in more than four hundred and fifty surgeries, and survived through hundreds of mortar rounds. I'd also received a Combat Action Badge, an Army Commendation Medal, a Unit Commendation Medal, a Good Conduct Medal, an Iraq Campaign Ribbon, and a Global War on Terrorism Medal. I could do this.

And yet, the thought of talking to a woman *still* made me so fucking nervous. David had warned about this feeling. He called it "approach anxiety, a fear of being rejected." A coward dies a thousand deaths, Hemingway had once said, but the brave man only one. That seemed to apply to dating as much as war.

Don't be such a wussy, I chastised myself. I took a couple of deep breaths.

I walked over.

I gently touched the small of her back (*touching is supposed to be a sign of dominance*), and she turned around. I leaned in (*breaking people's personal boundaries shows that I own the world*), and I whispered in her ear, "I know this may sound weird, but I just had to come over and tell you that you have the sexiest calves in this entire club."

She looked curiously at me but said nothing.

"That's all." I stood up straight. "I just didn't want to leave this club without you knowing that." I turned around as if to walk back toward David. The turn was a fake turn that David had taught us. It was supposed to give people the impression that we weren't really hitting on them, just giving a genuine compliment.

"Wait! Don't go." She smiled. "Stay a minute."

I glanced over at David. He shot me a goofy smile and a thumbs up.

I felt like an idiot for using his tricks, but—what the hell?—it seemed like they were working.

"How about you buy me a drink?" she asked.

I pulled up a chair. "How about I just give you a sip of my beer?"

She laughed. I smiled. It seemed like forever since I'd heard a woman laugh—unless you counted the anesthetic giggles of a child while you're removing a bullet from an arm. The sounds are surprisingly similar.

Ten minutes later, the girl was jumping off my lap and hurrying away.

David came running over. "What happened?"

"I told her I'd just gotten back from Iraq, and then she said, 'Oh… are we still over there?'" I was breathing deep. "*Are we still over there*, can you believe it? So I was like 'Yeah, we're still over there, you fucking bitch!'"

"Ouch." David grimaced.

Our unit was the most investigated unit in the entire country of Iraq. The Criminal Investigation Division (CID) and Inspector General (IG) had multiple investigations happening simultaneously, for everything from mail fraud to bribery to abuse of power and dereliction of duty—there were even rumors of mercy killings. Halfway through our deployment two command sergeant majors, one first sergeant, and our company commander were relieved of their duties. But not Sergeant Doff. He was awarded a Bronze Star, because they all couldn't be scapegoats, could they? He was what people back home—with a straight face, because they wouldn't know any better—would call a "hero."

"This is fucking pointless," I said.

David placed his hand on my shoulder. I shook it off.

"Why did I think having a girlfriend would make me feel any better?"

People were starting to look. I ignored them.

In instances like this, mixing Vicodin and beer can be a good thing; when combined, they give you short-term memory loss, which helps when you're looking to forget things. In twenty minutes I'd nearly forgotten about the girl, and David and I were standing in the back of the club next to the velvet rope of the VIP section. "Act cool and be ready," I said to David. "This used to work when I was stationed in Texas."

I sauntered up to the bouncer standing in front of the VIP entrance.

"Excuse me," I said while trying not to sound drunk, which somehow always made it worse, "but I just saw some guy headbutt another guy, a guy in a red shirt." I pointed to the closest guy in a red shirt. The bouncer arched his brow and pointed to the same guy. I nodded and said, "Yeah, that's him." The bouncer nodded back, spoke into his radio, and headed toward the guy in red.

"Quick," I said as I waved to David, Bob, and Jarrod. I unhooked the velvet rope, and the three of us ducked into the VIP section. Set back between two large marble pillars and decorated with several faux-classical statues, black couches, pink feather boas, and stone tables, the room reminded me of how a pimp might have decorated a bedroom in ancient Rome. I sat down on a plush-satin couch next to three blondes. I looked past all the décor and saw a young guy sitting on a couch surrounded by beautiful women.

"What's the deal? Who the hell is that guy?" I asked.

"Oh my god," a blonde said as she tossed her hair. "Are you kidding me?"

I took a sip of beer. "Nope."

"Um… he's Jesse McCartney."

I glanced at Jarrod and David; they both shrugged.

"Not ringing a bell."

"Um… the singer?" Her eyes widened. "His albums are H-O-T. The DJ's playing one of his songs right now." She was clearly annoyed by our ignorance. "Have you been living under a rock? Does 'Beautiful Soul' ring a bell? It went, like, platinum. Hello, he won, like—"

"Okay, okay." I threw my arms in the air. "I get it. Yeah, I remember him now."

One of the things David had taught us was that men should attach themselves to other high-profile men. It was about social status, he'd said. I stood up and started walking across the room. "Hey, McCartney. I really like that one song of yours—I think it's called, 'True…'" I yelled, immediately confusing him with the singer Ryan Cabrera.

He looked up from his sea of women. "I think you're thinking of a different—"

"No. It's you, man—"

"—singer."

I lit up a butt. "That's a great song. I even tried to learn it on the guitar, in Iraq."

"Whatever, man. I'm not Ryan Cabrera. But hey, do you mind if I bum one of those?" He pointed to my cigarette. I looked at the hot brunette with him. She was what the class would call a "HB10"—and you can probably guess what that means.

"That's very cool, man," McCartney said as I handed him my last cigarette. He turned from me and back to the women.

"Let's get out of here," McCartney said to the girls. They didn't even look over at me. Before I could use any more of David's lines, before I could even finish my cigarette, the singer and the girls were on their way. I felt like I was drifting really fast. Then I looked back to the satin couch; even the three blondes had left. God knows what time it was, but I was the only one in the room. Even Jarrod, Bob, and David had gone.

6

Two days after my last class with David, I met Stephanie. She had been sprawled out in the park, thumbing through a worn-out copy of *Long Walk to Freedom,* by Nelson Mandela. I knew I had to ask her on a date. Tall and thin, with brown untroubled eyes, she had delicate, pale skin, tiny ears with huge dangling earrings, and full lips that moved as she read. My "approach anxiety," as David had called it, was gone. After a weekend with him and the other guys, talking to women now seemed like no big deal—or less of one, anyway.

By the second day of David's class—which mirrored the first (though it featured fewer fights)—things had started to click. I had "untapped game," David said, and a dark aura that could be sexy— as long as I didn't let it get out of hand with drinking and Vicodin. And he may not have been entirely wrong. When I went up to

Stephanie at the park, I had introduced myself as a fan of the book, and within minutes I had her number. She knew nothing about me, nor I her, but now there we were.

"So tell me about yourself," she said.

I didn't know where to begin. So she did.

She was an economics major and senior at San Diego State University; originally from Salt Lake City, she came out here because she wanted to be closer to the ocean. She loved country music and surfing, and she spoke of both with a reserved, almost religious demeanor. After a few minutes of conversation, she discovered that I was a war vet. "Oh my God," she gushed, "I like, love military men." And then slightly blushing, she asked, "So, if, like, we went on another date… could you wear your uniform? That would be so hot."

I had no idea how to respond.

She filled the silence. "Not that what you're wearing now is bad or anything. Your shirt is, um… nice."

It wasn't exactly the compliment I was hoping for, especially considering that since coming home I had spent more than three thousand dollars on clothes. Jeans, shirts, nice shoes, and a leather coat that cost almost as much as my first car. It was a shopping spree I had long dreamed about. Growing up in a working-class family, the youngest of seven, my entire wardrobe had consisted of hand-me-hand-me-hand-me-hand-me-downs. At one point, I even had to share the clothes with a sister who was *developing* as a woman and simultaneous going through a tomboy phase. Often she'd grab a shirt, wear it, and then put it back without washing it.

This meant that most of my shirts were left with nipple indentations, which was bad news for me. My friends loved it, though. "Hey Nip," they'd yell. "Cold outside?" "Trying to hide M&Ms in your shirt again?"

Stephanie pushed at the silence. "So could you…"

"Um … No." We were at a dense outdoor café, littered with chairs, tables, and patrons. The ocean was close enough that we could taste the salt on our tongues and feel the chill of the evening settling in. "I don't have my uniforms anymore."

It was a lie. My uniforms were all back at my brother's place, crumpled in a ball in my duffle bag. But I figured I'd do Stephanie a favor. When a woman pictures a man in uniform, the uniform isn't dirty, ragged, and blood-stained. There's nothing *hot* about that.

"I still have my dog tags, though." I exposed the chain from beneath my shirt.

Ten minutes later, we were in the backseat of her car and listening to a Toby Keith CD. "American Soldier" played in the background while she pushed her lips into mine. I pressed back against hers and forgot for a moment. Forgot where I was. Where I'd been. How I felt.

But then she pulled away.

"How was that?" she asked.

"Good," I said. "It was good."

My thoughts were fraying. Always, at this point. I couldn't hold them together, even when I wanted to. And I couldn't tell where they were going to go next.

Tonight the thoughts were about how to end things, with a

heavy emphasis on the *how*. The process of suicide isn't exactly easy. It takes preparation, scheduling, and a certain level-headedness to kill yourself. A person has to be ready for it. He has to make the necessary plans, take the necessary steps. And, most importantly, he has to not only feel like dying, but also like killing. And the two feelings couldn't be more different.

A successful suicide doesn't just *happen*, although, of course, there are exceptions. Someone happens to be walking across a bridge when the feeling hits. Or they're on the roof of a building and realize they have nothing to live for. But most of the time, suicide takes planning. That's the way I figured. The way I was figuring...

And then Stephanie reached for my zipper.

Cut to a very short time later. She was rising up again. "It's been a little while for you, huh?"

Heading into our date tonight, I had been hoping sex—if it came to that—would chase away these kinds of thoughts. I was wrong. She leaned forward for what I assumed was a kiss. My eyes went to her lips. David, unfortunately, hadn't covered how to handle this situation in his seminar.

I jolted backward.

She jolted backward too, surprised. "I wasn't going for a kiss." She wiped her mouth again. "My phone is behind you. I wanted to see what time it is."

"Oh."

She grabbed her phone. "It's getting late, and I have class in the morning."

"Okay."

"Do you need me to drop you off?"

"Yeah, sure."

The truth was I didn't want the evening to end. Even though I wasn't crazy about Stephanie, I had nothing else to do. The few moments we talked were good. Unlike that girl at the club, she at least knew our country was still at war.

But what could I talk to her about? My twelve months in Iraq? The people who died in my arms during surgery? The times I almost died during mortar attacks, operating as the hospital actually shook, or part of it collapsed? Crade's two suicide attempts from the stress of war, or Doff's dereliction of duty? Or the fact that I couldn't eat fried bologna anymore because the smell reminded me of flesh being cauterized? Or maybe how I had read Mandela's *Long Walk to Freedom* while in Iraq, which made me refuse to follow a silly order, which almost got me thrown in jail? Or maybe how I was thinking about killing myself?

But no, none of that would work.

Even the most patriotic don't want to know the truth about war. The truth about people.

If David had taught me anything, it was that in dating, less is more.

"Where should I drop you off?"

I looked out the window as we drove. A group of homeless people was loitering outside a liquor store. One of them wore an earth-toned coat with army patches. He was passing around a bottle with the other guys. They seemed to have the right idea.

"Here's good."

"What? Do you even know where we—"

"I'll be all right."

"Are you sure?"

"Yeah. Just let me out."

The light turned green, but the car didn't move. "Okay. So, are we going to, like, I don't know, talk again or something?"

I swung open the car door, mumbled, "I don't know," and stepped outside. A putrid smell hit my nose; I deeply breathed in the smell of car exhaust, garbage waiting to be hauled away, and a hint of cigarettes. I headed for the liquor store.

A cloud of smoke pooled beneath the store awning. All of the homeless guys had left, except for the one in the army coat. He was still there. He had had his hand wrapped around a paper bag, and he was leaning against the wall, one foot kicked up like James Dean in *Rebel Without a Cause*.

My plan was to grab a bottle of something and another pack of cigs and wander the city, but as soon as I passed the guy in the army coat, I couldn't take another step. The man's face was stop-you-in-your-tracks ugly. Grisly and sunken, with stress lines dug in like old trenches; his skin looked thin enough to peel back.

He really was a vet, I could tell. He wasn't just wearing the coat. Instead of continuing into the store, I leaned on the wall next to him. I lit a cigarette, cleared my throat, and held the pack in his direction.

He nodded.

I handed him the one I'd just lit while lighting another for myself.

He started taking quick drags, like it was a race.

"How 'bout an extra one, for the road?" he asked between puffs.

I was down to six, but that would be enough.

After a long, slow drag, I exhaled smoke and asked, "What branch?"

He put the extra cig behind his ear and said, "Army." Then he asked, "You in?"

"Just got back."

He muttered a few quick things about being in Vietnam, how he was infantry and had volunteered. After a moment, he exhaled a puff of smoke and stopped talking.

I stared at the ground and tried to think of something to say. I thought of telling him "thank you," but I didn't feel like it, and I hated it when people said that to me. Besides, I had no idea what the fuck he actually did over there. We're not all heroes. He could've joined in the My Lai massacre for all I knew.

"Iraq?" he asked.

"Yeah."

"Uh huh."

We kept dragging our cigs, him hitting his hard and fast, me long and slow. Neither of us said anything else. We were just there, as though all we needed to say had been said. I finished first. Long drags always make a cigarette go quicker. Sometimes I can do a whole cig in just one or two breaths, but only if crunched for time.

This guy was looking at the moon.

I took two more out of the pack, lit both, and handed one over. He snatched it as though I might pull it back.

"You from around here?" he asked as we finished our seconds.

"Nah, Massachusetts. Just here killing time."

"Uh huh."

He glanced over his shoulder and stared toward the nearby ocean. The waves were cascading down and sending a breeze our way. I could practically taste the saltwater. He breathed in deeply. "I've been out since sixty-eight," he exhaled. He lifted his shirt. His dirt-smeared skin was tanned a golden syrup, except for a white, pen-length scar on the left side of his ribs—a bullet or shrapnel wound, maybe. It was crudely done, probably by a medic in the heat of battle, rather than in a combat-support hospital. We wouldn't have stood for such shoddy craftsmanship there.

I opened my pack. "Last ones."

"Uh huh."

Two puffs out. "So what happened?" I asked.

He paused, perhaps unsure of whether I meant him or the scar. "The short version would be hooch," he said, and held up his paper bag. "And these." He gestured at his body with his cigarette. "I got discharged on medical. I was still a kid when I came home. No wife, no kids. I didn't know what else to do… so I drank."

I wasn't sure what I'd been hoping to accomplish, but listening to him was starting to annoy me. All I could think was how the war must've fucked him up too. And I didn't want to think about that.

The man turned his head back to the ocean. "Sometimes you

can't come back," he murmured to himself. "Right?" He turned back to me. I saw his hand trembling slightly, ash falling from the cigarette. "What's a good soldier look like to you?" he asked.

I breathed and was quiet for a long moment.

He echoed his question.

"What's a good soldier look like?" he pried. "Do you even know?"

I wasn't sure what he was getting at, but I knew what a good soldier looked like. I was only a few weeks home and I had served with dozens of them. There was Chandler, a hillbilly from Maine— he smoked at least a pack and a half a day and drank nothing but Pepsi. Sellers, a neurotic insomniac, who worked twenty hours a day, every day. Hudge, a Puerto Rican who got irritable bowel syndrome from the stress of war and was running for the bathroom as often as she was for bunkers. Torres, the Che Guevara lover and admitted communist. Reto, the emotional ladies' man. Denti, a lovable misfit who could quote every episode of *Family Guy*. Waters, the strip-club worker turned soldier. None of them the typical image, but good soldiers, nonetheless. Heroes, even.

"I can think of a few good soldiers," I said hesitantly.

"Bullshit," he said, oblivious to my growing annoyance. "Bullshit," he murmured again.

Something was clearly going on with the old man; what, I had no fucking idea, but I did have an idea of what made a good soldier. I knew that a good soldier wasn't a blind patriot. I knew that the opposite was true. A good soldier frees himself from his country, his constitution, and his unit. Every good soldier, from

Audie Murphy to Hugh Thompson Jr., has shown that the way to true heroism is through nonconformity.[2]

A gust of wind blew wildly through the street. I needed a break from this guy, from myself, from everything. I cleared my throat. "I'll be right back," I said, and went to get a pack of Camels and a bottle of peppermint vodka. In Iraq, peppermint vodka was all anyone drank. U.S. military bases in Iraq and Afghanistan were "dry," meaning no alcohol was allowed. But this rule was, understandably, often ignored. All it took to fool the military was a mouthwash bottle, peppermint vodka, blue food coloring, and a friend who was willing to prepare and ship the package from the United States.

We weren't all good soldiers, though. Colonel Lollydash certainly wouldn't qualify for the title. Looking out for his soldiers wasn't a priority; he was more interested in fabricating events so he could be awarded medals. Lollydash hardly even bothered to leave his desk. When it was time to open a new hospital, he ordered us to lie and say it was ready to open before it was, so that he and his cohort would look good—to get a promotion and an award or two. At one point in my deployment, one of the doctors conducted follow-up calls on some of the Iraqi patients whom we'd worked on. It turned out that most, if not all, had died. Even ones with minor injuries had died. What happened, he discovered, was one of three things:

---

2. Two of America's great military heroes (two of many). Audie Murphy received the Medal of Honor at age nineteen, and was one of the most decorated soldiers in all of WWII. Hugh Thompson Jr. disobeyed orders and helped end the My Lai Massacre. Too much to mention in a simple footnote. Take a moment on Google and/or Wikipedia for more info on these great men—and their own struggles coming home after their respective wars.

(1) We fixed the patient up and sent him to an Iraqi hospital that was run by a different Muslim sect than his, and he was killed.

(2) We fixed the patient up and sent him to an Iraqi hospital, and he was killed for merely being seen by the Americans.

(3) We fixed the patient up and sent him to an Iraqi hospital, and the patient died because the hospital didn't have the proper equipment or staff.

Hundreds of hours of surgeries. Days with no sleep. And, of course, the missed hours of sleep and meals were nothing compared to the loss of life. A dozen dead that we had saved. The worst part? Our commanders didn't care. Colonel Lollydash, a man who didn't work in the hospital, who had office hours and weekends off instead of blood on his hands, merely made a joke of it and told us to "keep up the good work."

I walked back out and lit up two cigs. Handed one over. Opened the vodka, took a swig, and handed that over, too.

While the vet took a swig, I thought about nothing. Literally, I thought about nothing. We were still young enough, me and my friends. For some of us, our lives before the war meant nothing. We had nothing. We were nothing. The older ones had wives, girlfriends, husbands, boyfriends, and children to return to, grounders to bring them back, anchors to keep them steady and in place. They knew what awaited them after the war. Even if things weren't perfect, at least they had something.

He handed the vodka back to me.

"Yeah, it was bad back then," he was mumbling. "But not as bad as it is now."

I nearly spit as I took another sip.

We had it bad? After all the stories I'd heard about veterans returning home from the Vietnam War, being called baby killers, being spit on, rallies against them and the war. There was none of that for us. There was nothing.

He took a drag from his cig, long and slow this time. "Better someone spits on you who gives a shit about the war, than to shake hands with someone who could give a shit less. Spitting on someone is passion. Shaking hands is s-so… s-so fucking…" he scratched his chin. "So fucking…" he repeated.

I took a drag and let it out. "Passive."

"Yeah. Yeah." He smiled. "People are s-so-*fucking passive* about this war." His smile faded as he took a hit of his cig. "But, it's, like, that's how it goes. You know?"

I shrugged my shoulders. He kept talking. I thought back to everything. Everyone wanted to shake my hand, give congratulations, and thank me for my service. But people didn't care. Not really. People really didn't care. People didn't know we were still at war.

I thought of *To Kill a Mockingbird.* I had finished reading it one night in a bunker, my knees bent and hunched together while mortars hit the ground, the glow of a cigarette and the moon as my only light. Standing there now, chain-smoking, I felt like I finally understood the ending. Boo Radley had saved the day, but he didn't want the praise that came along with it. He just wanted to be left the fuck alone. To thank him was to say nothing. It was the same for all of us. No matter what war we fought in.

I pressed a handful of cigarettes into the homeless man's hand. I wasn't in the mood to talk anymore.

"Thank you for your service," I said as I headed out.

He laughed. "Yeah. Fuck you, too!"[3]

---

3. At the time this took place, it was estimated that more than 200,000 veterans were sleeping on the streets of the United States each night. But thanks to civilian and military outreach, these numbers have been steadily decreasing. For more information, contact The National Coalition of Homeless Veterans.

7

Later that night, I found myself standing outside with Meghan—bright green eyes, softy pudgy cheeks that dimpled as she talked, and hair that was so black it couldn't be natural. I had seen her leaning against the outside of a bar with her skirt hitched over her knees. Clearly, she'd practiced the pose. She was smoking now and caressing my head with her free hand, her fingers warm against my scalp. I gazed upward as she massaged and tried to stop thinking about David Sedaris.

We'd been talking about books—about *Me Talk Pretty One Day*—but books seemed less and less relevant by the minute. She told me that she played guitar, which was cool, because I had tried to learn to play in Iraq, but then she told me I could have sex with her for a hundred dollars, which wasn't as cool. I only had ten left on me anyway.

"Military discount?" I asked.

She stopped stroking my head.

"Do I look like a fucking Denny's?"

She flicked her cigarette to the ground and stormed off.

I kept walking. Kept smoking. Kept thinking of Iraq. Kept thinking of how much I wanted to stop thinking.

I was reminded of all the prostitution stories that floated around base. From our interpreter (supposedly a prostitute), to rumors of female soldiers who went home with an extra ten thousand dollars in cash, to my personal favorite rumor: "If you're ever in Baghdad, go to the dry cleaners on base. Tell them your room number and that you lost a red sweater. They'll send a girl to your room." There was my command sergeant major who was supposedly spotted on leave with prostitutes. (He was later relieved of command for other reasons.)

I thought of Meghan, and whether or not I would've actually slept with her, if I had the money. After all, I had paid David a lot more than that.

No more than thirty minutes later, I was being escorted out of a bar by an off-duty cop working security. He asked me to stand on one foot and touch my nose.

"But I'm a *veteran*—"

I hated myself the second I said it.

VETERAN. It was my get-out-of-jail-free card.

Cops and soldiers are two peas in a pod. Both sides promise to risk their lives for the public. There's respect on both sides. And although the respect doesn't always flow evenly both ways, the cops, at least, tend to hold up their end of the bargain.

"Did you just get back?" he asked, hands hanging by his sides.

"Yeah. Army."

"I had a brother over there. H-he… got caught in a-an a-attack—"

He didn't have to say anymore. He didn't even have to clarity if "over there" meant Iraq or Afghanistan. It made no difference. His brother was dead. He let me go with a warning. "Just go home and sober up… and don't get into any more trouble."

I gave him a half-hearted salute—"Yes, sir"—and stumbled away. It was 3 a.m. and I was drunk, but I wasn't even close to being tired. Not that it would have mattered if I was. I'd taken an Ambien, but I'd abused them so often that they almost never worked anymore.

I kept walking. I needed to clear my head. I needed to get out of here. I needed to head back to Massachusetts. I needed to sleep. I needed to go. I needed to stop fighting. I needed to keep walking. I needed more Ambien. I needed somebody to knock me out.

I needed to go home.

8

We were in the kitchen of my brother Chandler's place. I'd just moved in. My mother asked me a question: "How was it over there?"

I looked past the plates covered in day-old pasta and meatballs and into the driveway. I could barely even remember the flight from San Diego. I wasn't able to bring my Vicodin on the plane, so I downed what I'd had left before the flight. I hadn't had anything to drink in twenty-four hours, and my left shoulder itched like hell. On my last day in San Diego, I had gotten a tattoo: *Know Thyself.* I barely remembered getting it, but some of the letters were raised on my skin, so something must have gone wrong.

"How was it?" she asked again.

Chandler was eight years older than me and had served five years in the Marines (he was recalled after 9/11). He had volunteered to go overseas during the recall, but his assigned job was stateside. I'd only talked to him once since being home, but I could tell that he regretted that fact. Not being able to fight, to go to war like his brother. And I couldn't blame him. If I were in his shoes, I'd have felt the same way. My whole family had worked together to fix up a room at Chandler's house so I'd have a place to stay once I came home.

Raynham, Massachusetts, a small town, thirty miles south of Boston—and the only town in Massachusetts to have a twenty-four-hour Wal-Mart, a flea market, and an adult video store. (Oh, the possibilities.)

My mother's dark-grey Hyundai Accent sat parked in front of the house, a small raised ranch with a brick front and off-white vinyl siding. I could feel her staring at me. Her blue eyes.

This was the first time my mother and I had been alone in more than a year. I could already tell it was turning sentimental, even clichéd. No soldier can return home without such a scene. And, of course, it was happening in the kitchen. Where else could it happen?

"You can tell me—"

"Tell you what?"

"Talk to me."

"About what?"

"About how it was."

"It was fine. I'm all right."

But I wasn't all right. It had fucked me up. Seeing people dying, listening to their screams, smelling burning bodies—everything together had fucked me up. Feeling the frustration of commanders who either didn't understand or didn't care that they were failing their troops—

I couldn't look her in the eye.

She knew me well enough to change the subject. "I thought you could use a good meal. I've got your favorites." She rummaged through a grocery bag. "Roast beef. Mashed potatoes. Sweet peas. Stuffing. And cornbread."

My stomach growled.

Or maybe it heaved. It was hard to tell.

I was craving a cigarette, but my mother didn't know I'd started smoking, and I didn't want her to know, although, embarrassingly, I reeked of Marlboros.

"You should have leftovers for a few days," she kept talking. "Give some to your brother, too."

My mother: a tiny woman, five-foot-one and a hundred pounds. She was a loving but tough, I-will-do-anything-for-my-family type. She had given birth to seven children, six of whom would join the military—three air force, two army, and one marine. She was a general of sorts, our commander, our leader, our mother. And even though we may have gone off to join the service, and even fight in a war, we were still just her kids. And I was her baby— *the baby* of the family. I looked at her hands as she unwrapped the roast beef. The letter I wrote her before I left for Iraq started, "Dear Mom and Dad." It was in an envelope marked, "If I die."

All soldiers were told to write that letter for parents, a spouse, siblings, closest friends. It was a letter that a soldier wrote hoping to somehow measure up to such a moment. To die at war meant to die for something. A soldier could only hope to earn such tears and remembrance. I had written the letters for everyone, not just my parents, but for my siblings and friends, too. Telling them how much I loved them. Hoping that my death didn't cause too much pain and that I died bravely. I had used my army stationary, faded grey with the army logo in the top right-hand corner. I used my favorite blue-ink Zebra pen too. In the military we learned to sign all documents in blue, to differentiate originals from the copies. I wanted everyone to know mine was the original. I wrote the letters two, three, and four times before I captured the kind of emotion that I hoped wouldn't be forgotten.

"I have to leave in a few minutes," I finally said. I gave her a half-hug, and I tried to kiss her on top of her head.

For years, my mother had been a seamstress at a dry cleaner. Her hands had become rough and dry from pulling and pushing needles, handling leather goods, clothes, and chemicals, day after day, year after year. She would need to be at work later in the day. She turned around. I started digging around the kitchen, making it look as though I was getting ready to go out. Maybe she might actually think that I had something to do or somewhere to go.

"Chandler and I will call you when he comes home." The truth was that I just wasn't in the mood to see her. To talk. To feel. To care.

After her car pulled out of the drive and into the street, I went up to my room and fell backward onto the mattress. I was tired, but I knew I wasn't going to sleep. My mind was flying. Drowning?

No thanks. Overdose? I didn't think so. Gunshot? Of course, I was kidding. No. Like an artist drawn to an easel, or a writer to the page, the proverbial light bulb appears overhead. I suppose that's what I was waiting for. That moment of inspiration. How should I end it?

Somehow, I drifted off. I dreamed of Crade and how he'd been in Iraq. I dreamed of the two times when he had tried to kill himself. I saw his round eyes and puffy cheeks. I saw him in the hospital, helping with surgery and cleaning the instruments afterward. I listened to him humming to the radio as he introduced me to new musicians like Gym Class Heroes and Seether. I saw him reading the *Satanic Bible*, the only book I ever remembered him reading.

When I woke up, I was covered in sweat and felt dizzy. I didn't move for a few moments as my eyes opened, and I looked around, remembering where I was. I checked the time on my phone: 8 p.m. I sat up in bed and grabbed my cigarettes. I cracked open a window, and a cool breeze moved through the room.

The walls still smelled of fresh paint, the bed sheets of fabric softener. In less than a week, the whole house would reek of Marlboro smoke. I grabbed the closest box and heaved it onto my bed. It contained all the books I had read in Iraq. Dog-eared, with broken spines, speckled with dirt, food, and even a little blood, most of the copies were marked up with notes in the margins. The better the book, the worse it looked—that's the way it should be. As I saw it, they were almost more like diaries than books.

I picked up a few. *High Fidelity*, by Nick Hornby. The main character kept incessant lists—"Top five songs," "Top five desert island records." By the end of the book I had my own lists. I asked people, "Top five foods you miss?" "Top five things you want to do when you get home?" People hated my lists, because no one wanted to think about everything they were missing, but they still played along. "McDonald's, cheap Chinese food, beer, Oreos, and real eggs," said one friend. "Get drunk, get laid, watch some TV, hang out with some friends, and get a new fucking job," said another.

The Zahir: A Novel of Obsession, by Paulo Coelho, which Jelleck, one of my friends over there, had given me. His girlfriend had sent it to him, but he hated reading and asked me to sum it up for him. Certain romantic sections had even been highlighted by his girlfriend, which I annotated for reference in his return letters.

Women, by Charles Bukowski. Combined with *The Zahir,* it was what made me decide to take the dating course, made me believe some sort of corny love story could save me.

Chandler was home now. I could hear him barreling up the stairs. I tossed the book down.

"Hey," he said, bursting into the room. He came in with force, but the cloud of smoke made him recoil. "Whoa. Are you smoking in here?"

"Yeah. Is that a problem?"

"No." He looked around. "I guess not."

"Okay. Good."

"What are you up to? You want to grab a drink?"

"No. I've still got to unpack. Thanks, though."

"You sure?"

"Yeah. Thanks."

He raised his eyebrows. "Jerry and Phil are gonna be there," he said encouragingly, as though his two friends were enough to sweeten the deal, and maybe they would've been, a year ago. I used to love hanging out with Chandler and his friends.

I stared down at my books. "Still no. But thanks."

"All right. I'll be back later. Maybe we can see a movie?"

"Yeah. Sure. Maybe."

His feet pounded back down the stairs, the front door slammed, his car sped off. I was alone again.

The duffle I'd lugged twenty thousand miles was in the corner of the room, lumpy and leaning against the wall. Everything landed with a loud thud as I emptied it: uniforms stained with blood, cold weather gear never used, flak vest without the inserts, knee pads never used, PT gear barely washed, sneakers worn out, socks and underwear spotted with holes. My eyes settled on my boots. When I had first been given them, they were a size too big. "You'll grow into them," the supply sergeant had said, echoing what my mother had repeated for years whenever we'd gone school shopping. He was right, though, just like my mother had been. I put the boots on. Caked with blood and one-inch heels worn down to a nub, they fit perfectly. I was done growing.

Next, I opened a box of paperwork. A DD214 discharge from active duty was filed on top, medical records were below, followed by a hundred insurance forms. In Iraq they kept losing our paperwork and we all had to sign and re-sign our insurance paperwork every few weeks. My family would've gotten six hundred thousand dollars if I died. Now, nothing. Underneath all of it lay my "If I die" letters. Although I was no longer at war, or going to war, they still felt relevant. Drunk drivers, serial killers, falling pianos—I could accidentally die before I had a chance to do it myself. The army had taught me to always be prepared.

I lit a cig and began writing a new one:

> Dear Mom and Dad,
> If you're reading this, it means I'm dead…

I felt less encumbered this time around. Less worried about what would happen afterward. I already knew how I'd be remembered: a coward. As someone who couldn't handle the emotional aftermath of war. The knowledge was at least freeing. I tried to think of good times to write about, but memories from before the war were becoming harder and harder to remember. The distant memory of a lone midnight kiss at a high school party, a family vacation in France, or a game of volleyball with friends, could hold no ground against the remembrance of a shaking hospital during a mortar attack. I ended the letter after three and a half pages. I made sure not to add the date.

9

I was thinking about the Episcopalians and how they said, "In the midst of life we are in death." I was thinking about Captain Tarr, an older nurse in Iraq, who had given so many blowjobs to so many different guys that the Marines had given her the nickname "The Viper." She always carried around a Bible and was always talking about Genesis and the book of Ecclesiastes. I often wondered where she put her Bible while fellating. One time, I even caught her while she was—

"Earth to earth, ashes to ashes, and dust to dust."

I was thinking about Sellers, one of my sergeants. She was a germaphobe. To her, microbes seemed more dangerous than mortars. She washed her hands before and after going to the bathroom. To even sit on the toilet, she'd use half a roll of toilet paper and build a nest. Anyone going to the bathroom after her was guaranteed either a clogged toilet or no toilet paper. Some of her habits even started rubbing off on me: I washed my hands before going to the bathroom as well as afterward, I never shared water bottles, and I always built a nest on a public toilet. Sometimes, in particularly seedy barroom bathrooms, I'd sit perched an inch or two high.

Leaning back on the toilet now, I tried to sit up straight, but every muscle was aching. My legs spasmed, and I realized that my muscles felt the same way after a night of drinking as they did after a workout. I tried to relax. Breathe in four seconds. Hold four seconds. Blow out four seconds. Repeat. I was thinking about a poem I had written the day before:

> *In the army, we learned to L.A.C.E.,*
> *To pivot and march.*
> *We did good,*
> *But now good was done.*
> *And done was never as good as doing.*

Suddenly, I grabbed the basket between my legs, but nothing came up. I heaved again and again—nothing. Nothing. My blue jeans were wrapped around my ankles and my ankles were wrapped around the toilet, filled with vomit or shit, or both. I could also smell the metallic tang of blood. The buzzing noise that made my head spin made my stomach churn. I could barely open my eyes, and anyway, all I could see was red.

My brother was supposed to be staying someplace else for the week, but someone was in the house with me. Twelve months in

Iraq taught me to know when I wasn't alone. It was an instinct.

A searing pain tore through my arm—

I forced my eyes to open fully. I abandoned trying to sit up. I continued leaning on the back of the seat. All the people in Iraq who were fucking. Prostitutes. Captain Tarr. "Earth to earth, ashes to ashes…" Why? What was the point? And why couldn't I stop thinking about it? I had no idea how long I'd been there, but from the smell, it had been a while. A door opened somewhere, closed, and I heard another toilet flush. I couldn't bring myself to get up and determine the identity of the mystery guest, but I didn't care much either. I stopped thinking of the Bible and instead started regretting the bottle of McGillicuddy's and the handful of Klonopin I'd polished off.

I picked my cigarettes out of the toilet paper roll (their arrival there the source of another mystery), and realized that I had no idea how I had even made my way over here from the couch; I began to think that perhaps the person I'd heard earlier was actually me. "From dust we come, and to dust we return." Again, I was thinking of Iraq.

A petite, scraggly haired sergeant had approached me one day with a question: "Anthony, what blood type are you?"

"O positive, sergeant." The most common type.

"Good, report to the lab. We've got incoming patients. Our blood supply is almost gone."

It happened a few times. Insurgents would attack our supply lines, and the hospital would run low on certain provisions. It was mostly harmless enough, and different sections would have fun stealing from one another. The ER would steal bandages from the ICW, which had stolen them earlier from the ICU. Every now and again, critical supplies would be down. Once, for at least a few hours, our hospital ran out of plastic gloves—a small but essential part of modern medicine. This time, we were running low on blood.

An hour after donating, I was scrubbed in on a surgical case.

"Clamp!" the doctor yelled.

An insurgent had been flown in by helicopter. He was littered with shrapnel from an explosion and was bleeding. "Suture!" the doctor yelled.

"We need more blood!" the anesthesiologist shouted at the nurse. "O positive!"

We had no idea where the patient was bleeding from, which meant a long fucking surgery. The surgeon and I had been here many times before, though. We had our own rhythm:

"Suction!"

"Clamp!"

"Suture!"

Repeat.

"Suction!"

"Clamp!"

"Suture!"

After a few hours, the patient had already died twice on the table, and we had gone through so much blood that I realized that some of the plasma had to be mine. Unfortunately, it was going straight through his body and onto the floor. The doctor had donated, too, also O positive, and had made a droll comment about us standing in pools of our own blood.

A joke, that's all it was to us at that point. And it had to be. If we allowed the talk to be anything else, we wouldn't have been able to do our jobs.

"Michael!"

I was back in the bathroom, a cigarette dangled from my lips. Someone was yelling my name.

"Michael!"

"Michael!"

We had to turn part of ourselves off. We had to, to survive. The only hard part was turning ourselves back on.

10

In California, I first discovered that a lot of the guys who gravitated toward "how to attract women" classes also tended to form up into groups. In cities all across the United States, in what were commonly coming to be known as *lairs*, men gathered together (sometimes in groups as large as twenty) to try to pick up women. David was only one of many such "gurus" who were teaching dating classes throughout the United States. And for the price of $29.99 for an ebook, $179.99 for a CD program, or two thousand dollars for an in-person weekend seminar, anyone could learn from these instructors. Students of these various gurus formed the basis of the local lairs, and—emboldened by the pseudoscientific techniques learned through classes, ebooks, and online forums—they would meet up and practice together—much the same way we had done with David two weeks earlier. Simple. There was even a formula:

Step one: Approach your intended target with
strong body language: shoulders back, chest out,
chin out, eyes straight ahead.

Step two: Engage your intended target in conversation. There are two general modes of possible
conversation. The direct method: letting your
target know immediately that your interest in
them is sexual. "You're beautiful, and I want to
take you home." The indirect method: make it
seem as though your interest is benign. "Hi. My
friends and I were just discussing [insert con-
temporary topic here] and I was wondering if
you could help us settle an argument?"
[If using the direct method, it's possible that
you've been slapped at this point; if that's the
case, rethink your approach. If your indirect
approach was not directly rebuffed, continue to
step three. If your direct approach was successful, however, skip ahead to step four.]

Step three: Subtly make the conversation more sexual, while trying to engage in physical contact;
i.e., a gentle touch on the arm, or even a high
five after a humorous comment. While engaging in step three, observe target for indicators of
interest (IOI)—smiling, laughing, playing with
her hair (with a baseline at simply continuing
the conversation).

Step four: If significant IOIs are found, enact
"closing game" protocols; i.e., ask for her number, schedule a date for later in the week, or
invite her back to your apartment for a drink.
(If no IOIs are found, disengage.)

The preparation, methodology, and continuous running of
drills that we all went through reminded me of basic training.
Just as soldiers learned to become proficient in learning how to
kill—with rifles, knives, and in hand-to-hand combat—so too were
we now being trained to seduce girls of all stripes. We knew (or
thought we knew) what to say if a woman was alone, or in a group,
or even hanging out with twenty other guys. We practiced opening
lines, honed our techniques for getting numbers, and even tried
to perfect the delicate art of the head massage. Lean, mean, sexing
machines, you bet—that was our service. We aspired to studliness.

"You need to get your shit together," David had said back in
San Diego. "You need to join the Boston lair when you go home.
I was there a few months ago, teaching a class. They're a good
community of guys, and that's what I think you need." He had a
point. Community was what I missed most about being in Iraq.
The friends. The sense of purpose. We were all embracing the suck
together. But this Boston dating lair wasn't really what I'd had in
mind—not at first, anyway.

Wolfenstein was one of the leaders of the Boston lair, and he
loved doing magic tricks. He would shout at women in a bar: "Pick
a card. Any card!" and after that, you couldn't shut him up. He'd

do this anywhere, in any bar in south Boston, on any typical strip. Even with music blaring, he'd give it a try. But it was best if the room was quiet enough so that we could hear one another for cues. It was better if there was room to move around in, too; better, but not necessary. Right now, Wolfenstein said we had come to the *perfect* place.

"Is this your card?" Wolfenstein pulled an ace from the deck.

"Oh my god," one of the women screamed. "How did you do that?"

He laughed and touched her arm. "A magician never tells."

Everyone in the Boston scene knew magic tricks, and none of them had real names. They all used internet pseudonyms—their "seducer" alter egos. Brad, a computer programmer during the day, would become "SammyFastFingers" at night. I never even knew what "Wolfenstein" or "Commando"—who was also there with us—had written on their birth certificates. Actually, they both looked like guys who might have legally changed their names to match their new personas. They were skinny, with their hair slicked back, wearing button-down shirts with the top buttons unbuttoned. And they used fake deep voices that made them sound like little boys pretending to be older than they were. They were both deeply weird—and not in a fun, ironic way. They were weird in the "why did you just lick that?" kind of way.

After I'd told them to just call me "Michael," they both rolled their eyes and said I was a "rookie."

Later that same night, after being rejected by a group of girls, Commando walked over to me and Wolfenstein to offer his accounting. "They all have low self-esteem. So no waste. Know what I mean, rookie?" That's another thing about these guys; they celebrated their rejections along with their triumphs. It was a numbers game to them. They'd ask a thousand women for their numbers, "because they all can't say no," as Commando had elaborated.

Wolfenstein ignored Commando and turned toward the bartender, "Can I get three shots for these lovely ladies?" He motioned to the three women he'd been entertaining with the card tricks.

He ordered three shots of Hpnotiq, and I had to laugh, because I knew what was coming. The girls didn't, and glared at me.

"Check this out, ladies," Wolfenstein said, as he took out a leather string with a heavy crystal dangling from one end.

He swung the crystal back and forth in front of the girls, claiming he could make one of them forget the number seven.

As the girls gazed at Wolfenstein and his crystal, Commando stood behind them, thrusting his hips in a humping motion. While the table was distracted, I downed one of the shots of Hpnotiq. Given the circumstances, it only seemed right.

That's when "Gunner" showed up.

"Commando. Wolf." He gave them both high fives.

Actually, Commando was doing me a favor. He had invited Gunner because he thought I would get along with him. Gunner had been in the army and he'd gotten back from Afghanistan six months before I had. He was tall and lanky, with wide eyes, a small Irish nose, and a weak chin that even a week's worth of stubble couldn't hide. He was dressed in the same preppie getup as Wolfenstein and Commando. But he seemed different. His eyes were softer, less predatory, and his voice, though deep and rough, was his own; he wasn't acting. The guys called him by his internet alias, Gunner, instead of his real name, Charlie. Other than that, he was more like me than them. Neither of us said it, but I could tell that he was in a similar boat. He wasn't out with Commando and Wolfenstein because he wanted to do magic tricks. He just needed something to do, something to focus on, to take his mind off the war, so why not get laid?

"You were medical?" Gunner asked.

We were sitting in the back of the bar. Roomy, casual, and quiet, it was easy to tell why Wolfenstein had liked it. Even when it was at max capacity, as it was earlier in the night, there was enough room to move around, and we were still able to clearly hear one another. Commando and Wolfenstein had left shortly after Gunner arrived. The women they had been entertaining—three tourists from Virginia who apparently loved Boston accents and magic tricks—were looking for a memorable night. Before leaving, Commando had asked if we wanted in on some kind of orgy. We laughed and declined, but it was hard to tell if he was joking.

"Yeah, I worked in the operating room. Helped doctors with surgery and stuff."

"Cool."

"You?"

His lips crinkled into a smile and he laughed. "… I was a gunner."

"Oh, yeah. Right."

"You must have seen some stuff. Being medical and all."

"Yeah, I saw a bit, just like everybody else, I'd imagine."

"True. I only put bullets into guys. Never took them out. Must feel good, saving a life instead of taking one."

Bone, bloods, and mortar fire. I didn't want to think about it and I didn't want to talk about it, either. Not with him, not with anyone.

A silence filled the air between us.

He changed the subject. "You've only been back like a month, right? I guess that's not much time. Still, how the hell did you get hooked up with those two idiots?" He motioned toward where Wolfenstein and Commando had been doing their tricks earlier.

We both laughed, relieved.

"I don't know. I thought it sounded like a pretty good idea." I told him about David, Bob, Jarrod, and Chuck. He then recounted his own experience. A different dating coach, a different group of guys, but similar enough situations, and with similar results. Bars. Drinks. Jealous boyfriends. Failed pick-up lines. And, sometimes, success.

"So how's it been being home?"

"It's been ..." I hesitated. "I don't know. I guess I just really don't feel like I'm home yet, you know?"

He took a swig. We were both drinking Jack and Coke. "Yeah... It takes a little while to *really* come home."

A girl in plaid pants and an oversized pink halter top walked over. Definitely a hipster, probably enrolled at Emerson. "Hey. My friends and I overheard you guys talking. You're veterans, right? Can we buy you a drink?"

Thousands of dollars on dating courses, and it turned out all we needed to do was let girls overhear us talking about the war.

"Maybe some other time," Gunner said.

That's one thing I'd already learned about Gunner. He was abrasive, at best, when talking to women. Earlier in the night, Gunner's one pass at a girl went something like this: "What's a girl like you doing in a classy place like this?"

But still, he had his shit together, to all appearances. He didn't seem too weighed down by the war. It was over to him. Finished business. And after two hours of conversation, I began to think that things might actually be okay. Maybe I just needed time.

Outside, we were smoking cigs and he was putting his number into my phone.

"Two thousand bucks on a dating course and the only number you get tonight is mine."

"It's better than having an orgy with Commando!"

We were laughing. He finished putting the number in. Afterward, we stood there for a moment.

He talked first.

"Let's definitely talk again sometime. Even if it's not to hit on chicks, which it seems like we're both horrible at anyways."

"Hey, speak for yourself. I would've done fine if I didn't have you badgering me all night."

He laughed. I laughed. There was another pause. He looked at me. "So, um, listen, man. There's something, I… I… I wanted to tell you." He put his hands in his pockets. "When I first came home, I kind of had problems adjusting. Those first few weeks, I couldn't sleep. Couldn't think straight. I was anxious all the time. I'm not saying that's you, but… Anyway, I've been taking Klonopin and Wellbutrin for a few months now. They've both helped."

"I'm fine, but thanks for—"

He took out a bottle of Klonopin. "If you wanted to give it a try… see if it might—" he dumped a few into his hand, "I could spare a couple… save you a trip to the VA, their waiting lines are killer. Took me a month to get an appointment—"

"Um, sure. Thanks, man." I grabbed the pills faster than I meant to and put them in my pocket. "I think I'm going to stay out a little longer, though."

"Okay."

"Is there another bar around here?"

Gunner had lived in the area for a while and used to be really into the "local scene," as he called it. He pointed across the street to a narrow alley.

"It looks like a fucking dead end."

He put on an over-serious expression and said dramatically, "Every road's a dead end for somebody."

He then took a drag of his cig. "But no, dude, there's a couple of dive bars on the other side."

"All right. But if I get murdered down there, it's on you." I flicked my cigarette to the ground and felt for the pills in my pocket. They were tiny; I wouldn't even need water. I crossed the street and passed a sleeping homeless man in the alley. He had a sign:

Vietnam Vet
Anything Helps.

I tossed a couple of coins into his little metal box. They hit with a ting and woke him up. He nodded his head and groaned gruffly before closing his eyes again. Then I downed the pills. It's the last thing I remembered that night.

11

Joe T's, just down the street from my house, was the dive bar to end all dive bars. A few pool tables in front, old cranky waitresses ambling around out back, cheap beer poured in water-stained mugs, and clientele that was drunk most of the day. It wasn't the best place to meet women, but it was the best place to go if you wanted to go out and be left alone for a few hours. Wilson agreed.

While serving together in Iraq—same medical unit, different jobs—Wilson and I had developed a love-hate relationship. He was a good enough guy, even if every now and again, he sometimes told a story that made you question his truthfulness. He was always talking about the time he worked as a drug dealer, or the time he dated a porn star.

"How are you handling being back?" I asked him. We were seated at the bar, beers in hand.

"With cocaine, man," he laughed. "You want some?"

I shook my head. We had our differences.

I had no problem chain-smoking, getting drunk, and popping Vicodins and Ambiens—but for whatever reason I had drawn the line at coke. Wilson took the opposite view, and had refused my earlier offer of Vicodin. We all had our tastes, I guess.

"Nah. No thanks, man."

We had our similarities, too. We both loved corny jokes. We both loved the board game *Risk* and hated to lose. And neither of us had ever been very good with women.

"Oh, okay," he said. "I've really only done it a few times since being home."

He trailed off, and then we both sat there for a few moments, sipping our beers, rubbing the labels, tossing peanuts into our mouths.

"But I used to," he was halfway through a speech before I realized he was talking again. "I'm telling you… I dated a porn star."

"I know, man. Congratulations."

We ordered two more beers.

"I fuckin' hated being over there."

We both knew we weren't military lifers.

"I wasn't meant for that goddamn uniform."

"I know, man."

"I love not having to shave. Not having to get a haircut. Not having to put up with all that bullshit."

This was how we went back and forth.

"Half our unit should've been kicked out. People lying to get awards. Stealing equipment. Capler gets caught screwing—"

"Oh man, you asshole. Now I have that image back in my head."

Talking about nothing. Mainly, we kept the subject to sex. Which meant that we talked a lot about other people and not much about ourselves. It often seemed like we were the only two people who weren't getting any action.

We ordered two more beers, switching to something cheap on tap. Bottles were adding up fast.

"Fucking STDs. That's why I never had sex over there," Wilson said, implying that he'd had a choice. "Everyone was fucking. It was disgusting."

I nodded in agreement, though it was hard to tell how much either of us believed what we were saying.

Wilson wanted to go to a different bar.

"He's coming, he said he'll be here."

"What kind of fuckin' name is Gunner?"

"I don't know, man. It's his internet name."

"His *internet name*? Jesus Christ. I knew there was something off about you. I knew it the second you gave me that book to read by… what's his name? Nobo…?"

"Nabokov? *Lolita?*"

"Yeah, that's the one." He sloshed his drink as he spoke, getting some on the guy next to him.

"Watch it," the guy said.

Wilson hardly turned toward him, "Oh, sorry," and then turned back toward me. "That was a weird fucking book."

That's when Gunner showed up.

Since the night at the club—only four days earlier—we'd gone out drinking every night. I'd learned a few things about him, as I'm sure he had about me. One thing I'd noticed was that although he was a liberal enough guy, and supported the repeal of Don't Ask Don't Tell, he was also the type who would consider it the worst kind of insult to be mistaken for gay. As a consequence, he made some subtle comment every time we met up.

"What's up, homo?" he said as he walked up to me and Wilson.

And yeah, sometimes he mixed it up with explicit homophobia.

More drinks. Before we knew it, the three of us were shitfaced.

"Three shots of tequila please," I said to the bartender, then turned to the other two with the follow-up. "And what do you guys want?"

Neither was listening.

"There's so many of us…" Gunner was mumbling to Wilson, "… think about it… so many fucked-up veterans that it's a fucking cliché… *We're* fucking clichés."

By the time the shots arrived, Wilson and Gunner were busy arm wrestling—a typical activity among drunken soldiers. As I looked on (my money was on Wilson), and watched them laughing and struggling, I thought about one of the interpreters in Iraq. He alleged that, during one of the periodic purges, one of Saddam's generals had specifically exempted an old friend of his, despite his being on the kill list. Just because they knew each other from their earlier days in the military. His advisors told him not to do it, but the general rebuffed their advice and let the man live.

And that was what a friendship was built on, whether you lived in the United States or Iraq. The bonds of war meant that even years later, when you're working for an evil dictator, hell-bent on genocide, you still have a soft spot in your heart for an old battle buddy, and that means you merely send him off someplace else.[4]

"Yeah, right. What a guy," Wilson was saying (after his victory). "I'd rather fucking die." Then he lifted his mug for a drink, but paused an extra moment before sipping, as though just then getting the point.

Gunner decided to tell us how he'd started volunteering at a center for post-traumatic stress disorder (PTSD) for vets.

Wilson and I looked at each other.

He understood the look. "No, seriously. It helps."

We ordered more tequila.

"No offense, uh, Gunner," Wilson started saying. "But I just got back after a sixteen-month deployment, and the last thing I want to do is to volunteer my free time with a bunch of fucked-up veterans."

"Me neither."

Wilson and I looked at each other. Neither of us fully grasped the irony of the moment.

Then it was last call. We were so drunk no one could drive, so we just walked to my house, which was only a few minutes away. We'd look for their cars in the morning.

"What's funnier than a dead Iraqi insurgent?" Gunner yelled as

---

4. Years later, I'd hear the same story about Hitler and a Jewish friend from his military days. The bonds of war, I guess, no matter how fucking crazy you are.

we walked up the street.

I looked over my shoulder to see if we were attracting attention.

"What's funnier than a dead Iraqi insurgent?!"

"Shut up, man."

Wilson was digging into his pockets, searching for something, but he paused long enough to play along. "I don't know, what?" he asked.

"Nothing." Gunner started cracking up. "Nothing's funnier than a dead Iraqi insurgent!" he screamed. We walked past dark row houses through a parking lot.

"Nothing?"

"Shut up!" yelled a voice from one of the dark windows of a row house.

12

A few hours later, I was up, sitting alone in my bedroom. A pack of cigs, a stack of books, and a tiny mirror by my bedside. I began talking to myself. Calming myself down. Telling myself everything was all right. I looked in the mirror. I was even thinner than I'd been in Iraq. My face looked gaunt, and I had dark circles around my puffed, bloodshot eyes. The reflection looking back was a sad one, a bit off center. One book I read said that you can tell a real smile from a fake one based on whether or not a person squints. Real smiles come with squinty eyes. Now, when I smile, I make sure to squint, too.

I lit a cigarette, and began putting on my shoes. The pants, shirt, and coat I had been wearing were still on, and my wallet, keys, and phone were still in my pockets. It was only 4:30 a.m., and I was all ready for the day, whatever the hell that would entail.

I went downstairs into the living room. Wilson was gone, which wasn't surprising. He was the type to just sleep over a few hours and then drive as soon as he was sober. Gunner was a whole other story. His shoes were kicked off and had gone MIA, his fly was unzipped, and a bath towel was draped over him. The blanket that I gave him sat unfolded on the coffee table.

I nudged him with my foot.

"Hey, wake up."

"… the fuck time is it?"

"Want to go for a drive?"

"Huh?"

"Come on, let's go for a drive."

My new car, a used Ford Contour—recently acquired for eighteen hundred bucks—sat in the driveway. It'd been over a year since I'd driven anything but a Humvee. Gunner and I got in, and we took off. Five minutes. Ten. Twenty. Thirty. Just driving around. Fuckin' aimless is what I was. Jobless. Hopeless. Just *less* all around.

When I left for Iraq, I had given my car, a shitty 1995 Geo Tracker, to Chandler. No radio, heat, carpeting, or even power steering. "A deathtrap," Chandler had said a few months later—after crashing it. He was fine, but the car was totaled. I had given my clothes away to Goodwill before leaving, too. It seemed easier to just give everything away.

Another twenty minutes. Thirty. Forty. Gunner was asleep, his head resting on the window, as I took the onramp onto the highway. Sixty miles per hour. Seventy. Eighty. Next was a series of back roads, main roads, dead-end streets, and then I started driving around the same rotary. I just started circling, and on the third time around, the early daylight collided against my eyes. I was repeatedly blinking, couldn't see a thing. The car visor, bent and broken, provided little shielding.

The sun in Iraq had never felt this bright this early in the morning. It would sit calmly in the sky and let you stare at it as long as you wanted. Sometimes we would do that, too—just sit and stare. A few friends and I made a sort of clubhouse on top of our hospital. We would chain smoke, strum our guitars, and watch the sun. Temperatures would rise to the hundred and thirties, and the sun would burn your body, but you didn't need sunglasses. Now, back home in Massachusetts, in the middle of winter, I needed to buy a pair.

Gunner groaned, "What the fuck, man?" and popped his coat collar in an attempt to block some of the sun.

"Wake up," I told him.

"Where we goin'?"

"I don't know. Where you want to go?"

He groaned again, reached over and turned on the radio, then leaned back against the window.

I had taken a few Vicodins. Now I could feel the blood drain from my face. The pills were making me feel heavy and wet, as though I'd been out swimming. I took them because they made things easier. I didn't feel so empty. But now I could feel nausea tugging at my stomach. I needed something to eat.

So I stopped at a donut shop and bought two breakfast sandwiches, an orange juice, and two chocolate donuts. Gunner thanked me for the food, but then right fell back asleep. He wasn't used to midnight dinners, but I credit the practice with helping me go from a pale, skinny kid of 145 pounds before Iraq, to a pale, skinny kid of 155 pounds while in Iraq. One friend from my unit took one look at my long, protruding German nose, bulging eyes, and generally gaunt features and started calling me "a Holocaust victim." After I gained the ten pounds, though, he revised his judgment and said that I looked like a survivor who had been taken in by the Allies. I took it as a compliment. Gobbling down my sandwich and donut, I wondered what that guy was up to now.

"I need coffee."

Gunner was up.

The days in Iraq tended to blend together. Yesterday was the same as today, and today was the same as tomorrow, and you couldn't remember exactly when something happened—only that it happened on a day like all the rest. Sometimes, it was hard to be sure if anything even happened at all. That's how today felt, too.

"I need some fucking coffee, man," he said again.

"Alright, man. I think there's a place close by."

"Comfortably Numb" came on the radio. Gunner and I both quietly tapped to the beat. Me, drumming on the steering wheel, him on his legs. Beats are somehow harder to resist when you're driving. If it were warmer out, both our arms would be out the window, either waving through the air or taping to the beat on the side of the car. Gunner turned the volume up. It was all done without thinking, really. Natural almost, and I thought about books, because they can do the same thing. A person gets a good one in their hands, brings the book closer, their thoughts focus, fingers flicker through the pages to the rhythm of the story—

"How's it feel being back home?" Gunner asked as we inched ahead in the Starbucks line. It was strange coming from Gunner— the fact that he asked the question at all. He was constantly bitching that people always asked soldiers the same stupid questions, including this one.

I shrugged.

"Well, don't forget about OK Cupid. It's what keeps me going right now. Seriously."

"You're pathetic," I told him, and gave the cashier my order.

Gunner had me take him back to my place so that he could get his car, but once we arrived the car was nowhere to be seen.

It wasn't in the parking lot near the bar, and it wasn't on the street.

At eleven, we figured out that Gunner had probably parked in a no-parking zone—or that his car had been stolen. We made a few phone calls and finally found out that it had been towed; he just shrugged it off. "That's just the fuckin' way things have been lately."

13

Samantha and I were sitting on the couch in my living room. We were catching up with one another. Casual. Chit-chat. My feet were kicked up on the coffee table, and she was sitting next to me cross-legged. She and I had been friends of friends and had gone on a couple of dates before Iraq. She was the last woman I had been with before leaving. She'd called me up out of the blue.

"You seem different," she said.

She'd only been here a few minutes, but somehow she could tell that I wasn't the same person. That I was *different*. And she was right. A person can't return from war and remain exactly the same person that he was before. But what was she getting at? What did she mean? And how could she tell?"

I didn't really know how to respond, so I just shrugged and flipped through a stack of old *Reader's Digest* on the coffee table.

The magazines were from my mother. Every year, she bought me a subscription. In Iraq, before I had even given my mother my address, *Reader's Digest* had started sending my monthly subscription. I always read them, too. Cover to cover. Month after month. In fact, I knew *Reader's Digest* so well that I once even caught a fellow soldier stealing a joke from an old issue. I called him out on it. When he denied it, I went to my room and dug out a previous month's copy of the magazine. Sure enough, the joke was in the "Humor in Uniform" section. Since coming home, I hadn't bothered reading them.

"So... how was it? I mean, bad, I assume. But tell me about it." Samantha repeated.

Here's what I thought. I realized how vastly different our versions of bad must be. When I first got to the war, bad was a twenty-four hour shift with no breakfast, lunch, or dinner and three dead. Toward the end, bad was when the PX ran out of Marlboro Reds and Camel Lights and I had to smoke Winstons instead, or God forbid, Newports, because I hated menthol. That was bad.

I lit a cigarette.

"So you smoke now?" she asked.

I took a long drag.

"Well... welcome back. You should be proud."

She smiled, and started telling me about a friend of hers.

"So, yeah, she was coming home from work one day... and a drunk driver swerved in front of her. And then some other idiot—texting and driving, of course—plowed into them both from a side street."

All three were sent to the hospital with minor injuries. Afterward, her friend had "found God"—whatever the hell that meant. It seemed ridiculous: all these people who found God after having a brush with death. A soldier in war had ten of those moments a day. By the eighth body or near-death experience, it was hard to care anymore.

"You know what I'm saying?" Samantha asked.

I had no idea, but I nodded anyway.

I took another drag.

She smiled. "You know, if you stopped smoking that cigarette, I might let you kiss me."

I took another drag. "I see *you're* still the same."

When I was in Iraq, I had spent a lot of time reading self-help books on the topics of women, sex, and dating. I wasn't a virgin, thanks to Samantha. She'd been the pursuer, of course. I had no idea what I was doing.

I thought that with a little time and guidance, I could return home a year and a half later as a regular Don Juan. But that experiment in self-education didn't come off as well as I would have hoped. There was little time, and less privacy. I didn't want other people to know about my personal project, so I hid the sensitive material, or else swapped out the jackets with ones from other, more respectable books. Once, during a lull in casualties at the hospital, I brought in a particularly graphic and descriptive hardback. I planned on reading parts of it during lunch, and had replaced the book jacket with the cover of Thomas Friedman's *The World Is Flat.*

That particular morning, though, I went to the bathroom and left the book on a table in the breakroom. It was only out of my hands for a couple minutes, but apparently that was enough. When I came out, an older male anesthesiologist had picked up my copy, and was casually flipping through and studying what he must have thought was the most graphic economics book in the world. There were quite a few diagrams, not to mention the sections I'd highlighted, as well as my own notes in the margins. I could see the confused look on his face. After a few seconds, he closed the book. I watched him study the cover, flip to the back, and look once more at the cover. Then he opened the book again and continued reading. I pretended not to notice. The doctor eventually returned the book to the table, but I was too embarrassed to pick it up and claim ownership. It stayed there for at least a few hours. The next day, the book was gone. No one knew it was mine, at least not that I knew of. After that, I tossed the rest of my learning materials in the trash. Now, here with Samantha, I was hoping I'd be able to recall a thing or two from the books.

I stubbed out my cigarette. Samantha and I kissed. Then we headed upstairs to my bedroom. A few minutes later, after we'd finished, she smiled at me. "We should do this more often," she said.

I nodded.

She started kissing my stomach, working her way down, seeing if I was ready to go again.

I relaxed against the headboard. *Life isn't so bad*, I thought.

But, on second thought, I had to go. I had to meet Wilson. It was an excuse, maybe, but it was true.

Samantha looked up and rolled her eyes.

I had once read somewhere never to give any thoughts, except your own, a second thought. And since then, I never had. We never should.

14

When removing a shot of tequila from a woman's breasts with your lips, it's impossible not to think about sex.

Her name was Maria. She was a lawyer ten years my senior. I arrived at her house in Cambridge for our first date, and we only talked for a few minutes before she took me into her kitchen. Once there, she sprinkled salt onto her left breast, squeezed lemon onto her right, and then had me take shots out of her cleavage.

"You're crazy, just like me," she said.

She poured another shot.

"I was expecting some uptight soldier."

I suddenly noticed that everything in her house was cow-print. Her wallpaper, the placemats on her table, the calendar on her wall—even the shot glasses were out of a Western.

"You ready for another?"

"Yeah."

People just assumed that soldiers were uptight, conservative, *normal* people. What folks failed to grasp was that soldiers can be weirdoes, too. In fact, a bit of insanity is part of a soldier's DNA. A person has to be a little insane to volunteer for war, after all. Even if for altruistic reasons. Maybe that's what Maria was picking up on.

"More shots!"

In fact, you can find every clichéd or quirky character imaginable in the military. I met several people from the country-country-country parts of the United States who were married to blood cousins. "There's a saying," they'd say. "Cousins are for cousins." The army was also full of prom queens turned strippers turned soldiers. In Iraq, there was one female soldier who worked in the operating room with me who worked at a strip club in civilian life. "I make more working at the club than I do working at the hospital," she'd said. If only the men stuffing bills down her thong had known she'd be fighting in a war for her country, maybe some of those Washingtons would've been Lincolns.

Maria grabbed a bottle of vodka out of the liquor cabinet. She lined up four shots on the counter, and that was when I knew I was in trouble.

"What made you think I'd be normal?"

She walked toward me, reached her arm around the back of my head, and grabbed a tousle of hair. "Before we do these shots," she gently pulled my hair, peered into my eyes, "I want you to kiss me."

It was hard writing a dating profile. Nothing seemed right, but it seemed easier to figure out what was wrong. I decided to leave out the suicidal stuff.

Maria was the first date of many via the internet. I couldn't remember much after all the shots, but what I did remember about the sex—which was rougher than I was comfortable with—convinced me that there was no chance in hell I was going back there. Instead, I decided to just keep going. I had six other dates over the next four days. There was Sarah, a petite interior designer looking for "the one." We had lunch together and she rebuffed my advances, saying that she didn't kiss until the third date. Then there was Angela, who was apparently a master of Photoshop. There were one-night stands: Lindsey, Mary, Ashley. They were all… nice. But none were able to take my mind off things. That was, until Natalie.

Natalie and I went on our first date on a Tuesday, our second on Wednesday, and our third on Thursday. We had slept together on our first date, and second and third, but it wasn't because of any magic tricks; it was because we had formed a genuine connection. We'd become friends.

Today, Friday, was our fourth date.

Her tall, thin frame was relaxed in the passenger seat next to me, and she was in the middle of a story about her friend, Gary, who she thought might be in the closet. "I can't just outright ask him if he's gay."

"Sure you can. I have this friend, Gunner, and he asks me all the time if I'm gay."

She laughed. "That's not the same."

"If you're friends, you can ask him. Simple as that."

She laughed and shook her head. She was twenty-one, in her third year of college, and willing to take things as they were. She didn't need to use Photoshop or some three-date rule.

"Don't be such a nerd. Just ask him."

The best piece of advice David had given me was that I needed to stop putting women on a pedestal—a line I was pretty sure he had stolen from a movie. He said that I had to treat women as human beings, as fallible, and as possible friends. They weren't far-off, unattainable, fragile creatures. He said to treat the girls that I met as if they were my guy friends. It was working.

It used to be the case that a woman like Natalie would've sent me running, stammering, unable to talk or think straight. Not that I was thinking straight at the moment, but at least I was able to talk.

"What are you looking at?" she asked.

"Nothing."

"Do I have something in my teeth?" She opened her mouth wide, brushed her tongue across her teeth. "Did I get it?"

"Oh. Yeah. You got it."

"Good. I mean, what if I met some good-looking millionaire tonight and he wanted to take me home?"

"He'd have to get through me first."

"My big, strong soldier." She leaned over, kissed my cheek, "But didn't you tell me that in California, you never won any of the fights you were in?"

"I didn't say I'd *stop* anyone from taking you home, just that he'd have to get through me first."

"He's going to have to work for it."

"Whoever this nonexistent good-looking millionaire guy is, he sounds tough."

"He will be."

"Okay. Good."

"But I do have a thing for wounded guys—so that might make it a little easier."

From the very first date, Natalie seemed to care about me, but not in a fawning, political, support-our-troops way. She didn't ask questions about the war or want to see my uniform. She didn't ask if I was glad to be home.

We were crossing the bridge into Boston. Holding my bottle of Vicodin in my hand, I was struggling to pop the top off while driving. I gave it to Natalie. "Can you open this?" I asked.

"Sure thing." She took the bottle.

"Thanks."

She rolled down her window and leaned out.

"What are you doing?!"

I watched in the rearview mirror as an SUV crushed the bouncing bottle of pills beneath its wheel.

"Tell you what—"

"What did you just do?"

"If you don't—"

"That was a new bottle."

"Michael—"

"I just bought that."

"Will you listen to me?"

"My prescription ran out, I had to buy that from this guy—"

"If you don't have fun tonight with*out* your pills—"

"Do you know how much this guy Zeke charged me?"

"—then I'll buy you *two* bottles!"

"You don't know how to buy them!"

"Michael," she rolled up the window. "I'm an upper-class white girl from the 'burbs of Boston. I can get a prescription for whatever I want."

I reached for my cigarettes.

"Touch these and you're going out the window."

She tried changing the subject.

"So I'm looking for a new book to read."

"Good. I'm not."

"I thought you liked to read."

"I can't believe you fuckin' tossed them."

"You know, Michael. You're such a fun, happy person."

"I don't know how I'm gonna sleep!"

"I can think of *something*," she smiled, "that will tire you out…"

We pulled up to a side street. She was still smiling as I parked the car. I lit a pre-dinner cigarette and she grabbed my arm as we started walking through Harvard Square toward a restaurant. The streetlights were on, and a sharp, cold wind blew as we walked. Along the road were reminders of a recent snowfall. Slightly melted snowdrifts, large chunks of salt, and puddles to slosh through.

"Hey, look," Natalie exclaimed, pointing at a "Free Books" sign by a table on the sidewalk. She stopped and bent down toward the basket. It was a take-a-book-leave-a-book type of thing. Probably started by a few college kids. I'd seen the bins in and around Boston before, when Gunner and I were wandering around drunk one night, but apparently it was new to Natalie. She immediately began rummaging through the basket. She grabbed two paperbacks, handed me one. "Now we both have something to read."

Mine was a detective novel. "Thanks."

She showed me hers, an old romance novel.

The truth was that I hadn't read anything, not even a newspaper or *Reader's Digest*, in weeks. I figured that since my three-month deadline was only a few weeks away, there was no sense in starting a new book. I couldn't see killing myself if I had a book that was only half-read: *Fountainhead, Catcher in the Rye, Hitchhiker's Guide to the Galaxy, One Hundred Years of Solitude*? No. I figured that those who killed themselves first had to finish whatever book they were reading… if it were any good, that is. Of course, there's always the occasional book that makes you want to throw yourself off a bridge just for having wasted your time reading it.

But I usually finished those ones, too.

15

The hypnotist, a balding misanthrope who had essentially charged me a hundred and fifty dollars for a nap, insisted that his CD would help solidify the positive messages implanted during our session. He told me to listen to it while I slept. He was ridiculous, but it seemed like a waste not to try it out. I fell asleep, and dreamed.

> *Voices screamed for help.*
> *People ran toward me through a dense smoke.*
> *Mortars began falling. The people continued running,*
> *screaming. Blue light streaked the sky and a whistling*
> *sound was followed by bullets and additional mor-*
> *tars. A breeze carried the smell of copper and burning*
> *bologna. I gripped the rifle tight. "This way," I yelled*
> *to the people, but they didn't hear. They ran through*

me instead, as though I were a ghost.
"Help us!" they screamed.
What can I do?
The smell. The sound.

I inhaled deeply and looked around. Darkness. Windows closed. Curtains shut. All that remained visible was an outline of Natalie's small curving back beside me. I thought back to earlier, to the hypnotist again.

His office had been in the basement of a building that primarily housed actual therapists. His room was wheat bread: dull and plain. A desk was littered with papers; there was a computer chair, a lamp, a small stereo, and a small couch. No paintings hung on the walls, and there was no sign of a diploma. The view from the lone window, of what I could only assume was a desolate alley, was blocked by a blackout curtain. After I told Dr. Haru my name, he took my money and asked if I had any previous experience with hypnosis. I told him I did.

October, my first month in Iraq. Routine abdominal surgery. Starting the second half of an eight-hour shift that had turned into a sixteen-hour workday. We were working on an enemy combatant. Cutting, cauterizing, and stitching; actually, it was quite boring. The anesthesiologist casually said to the doctor, "Hey, John, since things aren't too hectic right now, I've got this idea ..." He held up a book on hypnosis and explained that he'd been reading it for a few days. He wanted to try something out. A minute later, with the Iraqi insurgent still on our operating-room table, the anesthesiologist whispered into our patient's ear, "You love America. You love America. You want to kill all the other terrorists." The doctor loved it and, after a few rounds, he jumped in and started saying it along with the anesthesiologist. It was a crazy idea, but war can be pretty crazy. And after a few more rounds, I jumped in, too. We searched the body for shrapnel, chanting, "You love America. You love America. You want to kill all the other terrorists." Then the surgery was over, another patient came in, and then the next, and the next, and the next, and, as long as the patients were insurgents, we kept doing it.

"Interesting," the hypnotherapist had said blankly, as though his mind was gone from the conversation. I had meant to end the story there, but then I figured I had to at least explain the reason why we eventually stopped hypnotizing the patients.

It was the fault of two soldiers who were in charge of the MWR (Morale, Welfare, and Recreation) for our unit. They wanted to take our minds off the war; a Halloween party seemed like the perfect way to unwind. Music, dancing, nonalcoholic punch, and costumes! The day of the party came and one of my friends, Ellster, a big, broad shouldered, black guy, decided to dress as a gangster. Overall, it was a forgettable evening, and no one would've taken notice, or even remembered it, except for one thing. Around the same time as the Halloween party, there was a story in the news about a series of gangs that had been discovered operating within the United States military. As a result, the criminal investigation division of the army (CID) was put on high alert to look for possible gang members hiding in the military. One military organization on high alert +

one man dressed in a gangster Halloween costume = an official CID investigation of our unit for possible gang activity. It also didn't help that Ellster, "The Gangster," had been the third person in the unit to have an accidental discharge—a misfire of a weapon—which the CID was convinced was part of a gang initiation.

How did this lead to us stopping our hypnosis? Simple, really. Word spread that the CID was investigating our unit, and the doctors worried that the CID might stumble onto our experiment. It was an anticlimactic end for sure, but we had no choice. Paranoia tends to run high when you're attempting to secretly hypnotize a double agent.

"This is all very interesting," the hypnotist said. He clearly didn't give a shit. "But we really need to begin your session. You only paid for the hour."

"Oh, right, sorry."

He cleared his throat. "Let's begin. Count down from one hundred: One hundred, ninety-nine—" The words were rhythmic, relaxing.

The hypnosis we had done in Iraq was weird, and freaky, and it was all probably bullshit. I knew that, but after seeing a different doctor in Iraq hypnotize several people to stop smoking, I wasn't sure what to believe. The possibility that it might be true was what made it so frightening when I learned that David was going to be teaching hypnosis to guys like Jarrod, Bob, and Chuck. A Manchurian Candidate was one thing, but a Manchurian Seducer was a whole other worry.

"Everything okay?"

Natalie was awake now. I was sitting up.

"Yeah. Fine."

Gunner had recommended the hypnotherapist to help with nightmares.

"Is that your stupid hypnosis CD still playing?" Natalie asked.

"Yeah."

"You mind turning it off? It's annoying."

"Sure, I don't think it works anyway."

16

Chirping. Something was fucking chirping and it wasn't a bird.

"...the fuck is that...?"

Natalie stirred next to me.

"My phone," she groaned, and after a second of fumbling around, the chirping stopped. She rolled over and snuggled into the spot between my shoulder and chest.

"What are we going to do today?" she asked.

It had been forty-eight hours since she'd thrown away my Vicodin, and the last two nights I'd barely gotten any sleep. It took a few minutes before I was able to respond.

"I'm supposed to hang out with Gunner."

"Yes. Gunner and..."

"And?"

She raised her head and looked up at me. She smiled, as though

I was missing something. My eyes were barely open, and I tried to ignore the glance, but I was attempting the impossible.

"Gunner… and…?" she repeated.

"I'm hanging out with Gunner and… you?"

"Yes, I'd love to."

"So when are we meeting him?" she asked.

One of the other things about being off Vicodin for forty-eight hours was that I'd been moody as hell. I'd lashed out at her twice and almost called her a bitch, but I couldn't even remember why after the fact. She seemed to brush it off somehow. Each time it'd taken a pack of cigs for me to get my head straight enough to realize what I'd said. My index and middle fingers had been stained brown from the smoke.

"I just woke up. Can I just lie here for a second… Jesus Christ… I don't know, five-ish. We're meeting at Joe T's down the street."

"All right, Michael."

She pulled herself closer and kissed me. It was almost a question.

We laid in bed afterward, naked, panting. She picked a book up off the nightstand. It was the one from the bin in Boston. A murder mystery. Some retired detective, some unsolved crime.

"Was it good?" she asked.

"It was all right. Two stars."

She put the book back on the nightstand, tossed her legs over the edge of the bed, and got up. "Okay, let's get a move on."

Getting together with Gunner and Wilson was becoming a thing over the last few weeks. Meet, get drunk, and complain. It felt good to drink and talk and laugh with them, but it still wasn't enough. The thoughts were still there. The deadline. I imagined myself as a barrel with a hole at the bottom. I could fill it with laughter and books and friendship and sex but everything, inevitably, would drain out. Always.

"It's just so pointless," I complained, as I put on my socks. "And I don't even know why they want to hang out with *me*. I'm no fucking fun."

I had been thinking lately about the people in the towers on 9/11. The ones who had jumped from the buildings rather than be burned alive. Were their deaths considered suicides?

"Oh stop it, Michael. You're fun, and you probably inspire them. Look how well you're doing for yourself."

I looked around my room, unsure if Natalie was kidding. My army gear and books from Iraq, which I unpacked so many weeks ago, were still flung about the room. Other boxes were unpacked. Everything smelled of stale cigarettes: the curtains, the sheets, my clothes, my breath. And I was still unsure whether or not I should kill myself in two weeks.

I lit up a cigarette.

"I'm a fucking inspiration."

Natalie stopped putting on her pants, looked over and smiled, as though she knew something about me. "You are, Michael. You just don't know it yet."

Gunner was complaining when we got there. The girl he'd been dating had broken up with him.

"It's bullshit," he said.

We were at Joe T's, all of us sitting in a line at the bar: Gunner, Natalie, Wilson, and me.

"You know what I'm saying?" he asked Natalie.

His face remained expressionless, yet his eyes told his story. Depressed soldier. I looked over at Natalie. She was staring at Gunner as he talked. She put her hand on his arm. "You know, a lot of girls have a thing for wounded-seeming guys. You've got that going for you."

A good-looking girl in a short skirt walked by. Gunner turned to her. "Hey, sexy."

She ignored him. That was how things had been going. It wasn't all his fault, though. Gunner's problems with women had to do with math. Since he needed four beers before he was able to approach, or even talk to a woman, and since most women needed six beers before they could stand him, it all added up to some very serious drinking. By the time he was four beers deep, most women were on their first, and by the time they were at six, he was at ten. Tonight, the math wasn't in his favor.

Wilson wasn't listening or paying attention to either Gunner or Natalie. Instead, he elbowed me in the ribs as a girl with huge breasts walked by. "God works in mysterious ways," he said.

We ordered more drinks and another round of appetizers. Natalie had found a natural rhythm with Gunner and Wilson and I—and it certainly didn't hurt that she bought the first two rounds.

She laughed and complained like the rest of us. And she even offered dating tips to Gunner and Wilson. Things were going well.

Then Wilson barged in. "You think that's bad?" They'd been talking about online dating sites, so he clearly had no idea what was going on. "Back when I was in Iraq, I was doing guard duty one day, patrolling around the edge of the base, and I came across a pile of blood and placenta, right there on the ground—"

"Where do you come up with this shit?"

"It was an aborted fetus."

Natalie looked sick.

Wilson speculated that some soldier made the choice to abort rather than be sent home. Three women in our unit alone were sent home for being pregnant—the U.S. military isn't going to leave a pregnant soldier in a war zone, after all. Then again, with Wilson, the truth always seemed far off. He leaned back on his stool, almost tipping over, and closed his eyes. Months ago, we'd been soldiers together, proudly serving our country and saving lives. And now— Wilson opened his eyes and belched loudly—it was clear that we weren't the same people that we were on active duty. All we had was talk.

Later, when Natalie returned from the bathroom, she ignored Wilson and Gunner, and sat on the stool next to me. Gunner and Wilson were both clearly annoyed by this, since it forced them to talk to one another. It wasn't more than a few minutes before Gunner stood up and came over to me and Natalie at the end of the bar.

"Hey, man. There's three girls over there, gimme a hand. After all, the best way to get over one girl is to get under two more, right?"

Wilson cleared his throat.

"Come on. You're a ladies' man now, right?"

Wilson cleared his throat again.

"Come on," Gunner pried, still ignoring Wilson, "be my wingman."

Gunner knew I had neither the desire nor the skill to help with such an endeavor, but he still expected me to come through for him. It was a compliment of sorts, but still a nuisance. He got the drift, and changed the subject.

"I feel like getting fucked up tonight," he said.

"I don't have any Vicodins left on me," I told them.

Gunner put his hand on my shoulder, and he did so in a way that reminded me that he was very drunk and on antidepressants, but it was still sweet, in a brotherly sort of way. "I've got some."

Natalie didn't miss a beat. "*Don't*," she pressed.

Wilson stopped himself. "Never mind." He chugged what was left of his beer and walked toward the bathroom.

Somehow Gunner and I, as always, got to talking about the war, which left Natalie a fly on the wall. Gunner was talking about his commander, who had invented firefights so that certain officers could be awarded Combat Action Badges and Bronze Stars. "One time," he was saying, "this captain went on a patrol with us. Totally weird for a captain, right? It was an unscheduled patrol, too. But our commander had told us to take him out, said the captain was about to go home and wanted to go 'outside the wire' at least once.

So we took this guy out. It was only an hour-long patrol, and it was calm as fuck, like as calm as it gets, which was good, because this captain would've been fucking useless in a firefight. Anyway, we return to base and, like two days later, the captain goes home. A few months later, we hear that the captain was awarded a Combat Action Badge for engaging in combat during that patrol. I mean, *fucking bullshit*, right?"

Of course it was bullshit, but in the military, sometimes bullshit just means status quo. No soldier wants to return home from war without at least one combat story, even if it was made up. The captain in Gunner's story might as well have been Lollydash in mine.

"But I don't know, man. I never felt like I was going to make it home... like I wasn't meant to," he was saying. He was looking at Natalie, but speaking to me. "Maybe it was... fate... But, I don't know... screw God's plan, right?"

I worked out the thought in my head: If God created everything, and if man is created in God's image, and if man can dream a fate greater than the one set out for him by God, could God dream a fate greater than his own?

I had gotten into all sorts of philosophy stuff towards the end of my deployment. It all started when I forgot my own birthday—my twenty-first. That got me thinking, for some reason—about time, about life and death, and about, I don't know, *meaning*. So I started reading Nietzsche and Sartre and Rousseau. After a handful of books, though, I was no closer to any deeper meaning. If anything, I was just more convinced that everything was meaningless. The war. The people dying. Me. Us. Them. We'd been fighting wars for ten thousand years, and I'm not sure anyone could make a convincing case that it meant anything at all. Jane Goodall wrote of chimps fighting wars over territory; the Bible spoke of angels fighting against evil. Scientists and creationists don't agree on much, but they both agree that we're destined to fight. It's in our DNA, and it's in our souls, if we have them. But just because conflict is a fundamental part of life doesn't mean that it matters.

Gunner and Natalie started talking again, and instead of joining in, I watched the clock. Wilson had been in the bathroom for eleven minutes. I wondered if I should check on him.

"You know what?" I heard Gunner raising his voice over Natalie's. "Just shut the fuck up."

The clock lost my attention. I turned to the two of them, tossed my arms up. "Whoa, buddy. What the fu—" But he apologized before I had a chance to finish.

Natalie was unfazed. "All I'm saying, Gunner, is that true love is out there for everyone." She shot me a glance. "So don't be afraid to go after it!"

Gunner shook his head; he wasn't in the mood. He stared down at his bottle as he spoke. "Yeah, and what if I do go after it and what if I find no one, and I'm alone for the next sixty years? What then? Huh? Friends and family will get married. I'll be stuck buying gifts. Years pass: children, birthday parties. At dinner parties, I'll be odd man out, forcing people to arrange five chairs around a table instead of four or six. Or, okay, let's say maybe twenty years down the line I meet someone nice and I've already given up on ever finding true love. Let's say the girl is a few pounds overweight, has frizzy hair and an annoying laugh, but at that point, I'm also a few pounds overweight and my hair is thinning and my laughter is annoying. Maybe then the two of us get married, and both our groups of friends will say, 'See I told you that you'd find true love. It just took a while.' And we'll smile, but we'll both know it's a lie—"

Something happened to me as I sat there listening to Gunner. I wasn't sure whether it was because I thought what he was saying was bullshit, or because it was true and related to me, or if it was the alcohol, or lack of Vicodin in my system—but, either way, I'd had enough. "Maybe you *should* blow your brains out, dude."

"What?"

"No, man. Just do it. I'm sick of listening to your bullshit."

"What the fuck did you just say?"

"I'm sick of listening to your bullshit. It's fucking endless." A fervor rose through me. "Either a person can handle being home from the war, or they *can't*. There's no in-between. If you're so goddamn depressed that you can't handle it, then just fucking kill yourself. Just fucking do it already! Nobody cares!" The words felt alive, rushing through my gut and gullet into the world.

Natalie tugged on my arm, pleading, "Michael, *stop!*" I pulled away from her.

"No, I mean it. We all have our own bullshit. I'm just tired of hearing about yours."

"What? So we can spend more time on yours?"

A hush had fallen over the bar. Everybody loves a drunken show. Gunner stood up, knocking over his stool. He glared at me, his cheeks red from the booze, eyes glazed. His face scrunched, and he looked like a child on the brink of a tantrum, as though he might start crying and pounding on the floor, though I had the feeling he'd just as easily substitute my face for the floor. "You know what…" he said calmly, "I don't need this shit. I'm out of here." He stumbled to the exit.

"Michael, he's not going to be able to—"

"Fuck him."

"You gotta give him a ride."

Gunner stopped in his tracks, turned around, and raised the back of his hand. He lifted his middle finger toward the ceiling and let it hang there. I'd been flicked off before, of course, but usually only for a matter of seconds—not too long, not too short. But this was insane. His middle finger just hung there. Finally, after about forty seconds, he seemed satisfied and finished stumbling out of the bar.

"We should go check on him," Natalie tried again. "Seriously. Michael!"

Taking a handful of twenties from my wallet, I threw them down on the bar. I ran out to the parking lot. Gunner's car was still there. I looked in the windows. He wasn't inside. I looked on the other side of the parking lot. Maybe he forgot where he parked—

"Michael!" Natalie yelled.

She was on the other side of the parking lot, pointing to the street. Gunner was walking down the middle of the road, stumbling back and forth across the yellow line.

He turned to us, a bottle in his hands. "You think I'm afraid to die?" he yelled. "Because I'm not!"

A car drove by, swerved, honked. Two more cars drove by, two more swerves, two more honks. Gunner flipped each of them off. "I'm free!" he kept yelling. "I'm fucking free!"

"Michael, please."

"I'm not afraid."

"Hey Gunner," I called out. "Let's go inside and get another round."

Another car started honking.

Natalie and I walked closer.

"Get out of the fucking—"

Natalie was almost in tears.

"Get out of the fucking road, man!"

"*Gunner,* please..."

"Move it, asshole!" someone yelled, and then flicked a cigarette at him as they drove past.

He kept dragging himself forward, taking a sip of whatever was in his hands.

We had walked far enough from the bar that the three of us were standing on a bridge now, a river underneath. Train tracks a hundred feet away. Cars still driving by.

"Charlie!" I yelled, trying to use his real name, like a parent.

"FUCK IT!"

His wide, bulging eyes locked with mine, and for a moment, I could almost see the war playing through his eyes. I stared back and knew exactly what he was going through. Our souls were fed from the same river of war. I was on the same bridge, ready and willing to die.

"I'm fucking empty," he screamed. "Free and empty."

Water rushed underneath the bridge, and cold wind blew against our backs. The three of us shivered. Walking home from the bar on other nights, I had come down to this bridge several times myself. Peering over the edge, chain-smoking cigarettes, wondering about the end. Whether or not I could jump. Whether or not it would actually kill me. I was sure he was thinking the same.

"Hey, Gunner, buddy. You've got to come back inside the bar," I said.

"Fuck you."

"One of the waitresses wants your number."

He turned away from the water. "What?"

"Yeah, dude. That's why I came out looking for you."

He looked down at the river, then back toward me. "Which one?"

"Um, the one with the black hair."

"Yeah, right."

"Not the one with glasses."

I stepped closer.

He was looking at the river.

"The one with the flower tattoo?"

"Yeah, that one."

He took another swig of his bottle. Vodka. Peppermint, I assumed. He must have gotten it from his car.

"She was asking about you."

I stepped closer.

He tossed the empty bottle into the river. "Tell her to suck my dick." He reached for his crotch, but the gesture threw off his equilibrium, and he wound up hugging the railing.

Natalie and I ran up and grabbed him, each of us wrapping an arm around a shoulder. We started walking back toward my house. Natalie wiped her eyes and told him he was an asshole, but by that point, Gunner had no idea what was going on. He didn't respond or try to defend himself. He just peered at her with his wide, bloodshot eyes, like a dog that pissed on the rug. He knew he had done something wrong; he just didn't know what.

The wind hurtled through the trees and down the street. Gunner leaned over and vomited. After a few heaves, we pulled him back to his feet. The wind carried the stench of Gunner's vomit along with us. When we finally got to my house—after Gunner had fallen twice and puked once more—Wilson was sitting on my porch, smoking a cigarette and looking pissed.

We strolled up, still dragging Gunner.

"What the hell happened to him?" he asked.

Neither of us bothered with an answer.

Wilson shrugged it off. He went upstairs into my room to pass out on the floor, Natalie went to the bathroom, and I dragged Gunner into the living room and dropped him on my couch. His eyelids drooping, feet dangling off the side, he tried to kick me as I flipped him over on his stomach, making sure he wouldn't drown in his own vomit. He opened his eyes and lunged toward a pair of nail clippers on the coffee table. "Can I borrow these?" he mumbled.

"What?"

"Can I borrow these?" he mumbled again.

"Are you kidding me? No, you can't borrow them."

He put the clippers in his pocket. "Okay. Thanks," he said, and rolled over, sleeping.

17

The interior of Gunner's car was crammed with old McDonald's wrappers and empty fifths of vodka, as well as crumpled lottery tickets. Everything smelled like pinecones, because Gunner had one of those scented trees hanging from the rearview mirror—a nice touch. Cold air was blowing from the heating vent, the radio was static, and the tires weren't balanced. Every divot or bump in the road bounced us around.

"Sorry about the mess," Gunner said, "but thanks for coming."

"No problem," I replied.

He had asked me to accompany him to a PTSD group for veterans. It was the last thing in the world I wanted to do, but after watching him on the bridge three days before, I couldn't say no.

I rubbed my hands together. I needed to smoke.

"And sorry about the heat," he mumbled, his eyes still fixed on the road. "I've been meaning to do something about it, but…"

My phone was vibrating; Natalie and Samantha were both texting. They both *really* needed to talk to me about something.

"This'll be good. This'll be good," Gunner repeated and glanced over. His eyes were glazed, and his smile was placid. He was clearly on something. I just hoped we wouldn't get stopped. "Yeah. This is really gonna be good," he said again.

I had no idea what he meant. What would be good? A bunch of vets complaining about PTSD? How was that good? I nodded and gave him a "Yeah."

Gunner had heard about the group from a friend of a friend, and before the night on the bridge, he had debated whether or not to go. I guess he just needed the push, because after waking up on my couch the next morning, hung over and pondering the night's events, he decided that he needed to go—with me. He'd asked Wilson if he wanted to go, too, but Wilson told him to fuck off.

We arrived twenty minutes early at a small church in western Massachusetts: white vinyl siding, big wooden doors in front, and a sign out front that read, "Come inside for Message." Gunner seemed startled. "I didn't know it'd take place in a fucking church," he said. The front of the church looked new, with wood and paint, but the side of the church was dilapidated. Paint was flaking, paneling was loose, the stained-glass window at the top of the church was cracked, and the shadows from the surrounding trees made it feel like we were walking into *The Exorcist*. Two guys in Red Sox baseball caps were standing around, smoking cigarettes. With square jaws and long, dirty-brown hair pouring out of their hats, they both had full beards and perfectly white teeth. They looked like brothers; the only difference between them was that one had a lazy eye.

The Red Sox fans finished their cigarettes as we walked up to them. No pleasantries were exchanged besides a "Thanks" when Gunner held the door open. We followed the brothers down a set of stairs to a room in the basement. The room was cramped with a dozen or so folding chairs in the middle, set in a circle. The last glimmers of daylight shone through the lone window in the room. Coffee, juice, soda, cookies, crackers, and cheese were spread on a table next to the door. There were two other people already there: young guys, mid-twenties maybe, and wearing cheap suits. They walked up to the four of us and introduced themselves as Clark and Raphael.

Clark and Raphael ran the group (it was only their second meeting). They were psychology students at some local college. Neither had served. As each new person arrived, Clark and Raphael went over and introduced themselves. Gunner and I headed to get something to eat. Our plates were stacked with crackers and cheese, and we grabbed cups of juice. By the time Clark and Raphael closed the doors, there were ten vets.

"Shall we get started?" Clark stood in front of his chair. He was directly across the circle from me, and Raphael was next to him, directly across from Gunner. "First things first. We'll all go around and introduce ourselves. We'll say who we are, what brought us here today, the branch of the military we served in, and the conflict fought in."

Raphael was standing, too. "After we introduce ourselves, Clark and I will tell you about what we hope to accomplish here, and then we can do some fun exercises. Any questions?"

"Yeah, I've got a question," said a man with long, grey hair. "I was told there'd be pizza."

Clark forced a laugh. "We just put in the order. It'll be here in a little bit. Any other questions?"

Clark and Raphael looked around the room as everyone shook their heads and sat down. Clark spoke, "Okay then. Let's begin. Who wants to start?" He motioned toward the Red Sox brother seated next to him.

"My name's Mark. I'm here because my brother brought me." He motioned toward his brother with the lazy eye. "I was in the Marines and served tours in both Iraq and Afghanistan."

Next up was Dean, the brother. Dean served in the army in Afghanistan. He came because he'd been having problems with depression.

After Dean was Joe, a Marine who'd served two tours in Iraq. Then there was Paul, another Marine who served in Iraq. Joe still had his high-and-tight Marine crop top, and Paul had a shaved head with a thick beard. They came because they were having problems with alcohol and anxiety. Then came Gunner.

"Hi... uh... my name's Charlie. I was a gunner in the army in Afghanistan, and... well, I'm not sure what brought me here today. I've been on medication for depression and anxiety, but I stopped taking it about a week ago, so... I'm not too sure—"

My shoulders and neck tensed as Gunner trailed off. All eyes were on me.

"My name is Michael." I smiled, but never before had it been more of a lie. "I'm here because my friend Charlie invited me." I stopped there, forgetting to mention that I had served in the army and fought in Iraq, but Clark and Raphael knew enough to move on to the guy seated next to me.

Lou had been in the army and wore a "Vietnam Veteran" trucker hat. He sucked on a toothpick and said he came because he'd had a drinking problem since returning from "'Nam." He claimed that his drinking was under control, but that he wanted to keep working on it, since his son was coming home soon from Iraq. He said he wanted to be able to help him in case he had similar difficulties. Next were Jim and Jackson, two other Vietnam vets. Jim was missing an arm; he didn't even have a stump.

About five thousand amputations have taken place in Iraq and Afghanistan; in Vietnam, more than seventy-five thousand men lost limbs. Medical advances and all. Nowadays, we probably could've saved Jim's arm.

The man with long, grey hair, who asked about the pizza, said he'd also been struggling with drug and alcohol addiction. Last, but not least, was Ted, or "Teddy," as he told us to call him. When he'd taken his seat, in between Jackson and Clark, he'd drawn his chair back about three feet away from the group. None of us took offense, because the guy was bursting with muscles and was about as wide as a small car. His breathing was loud and heavy as he spoke. I'd seen a few bodybuilders who breathed like that. I'd been told that it meant they'd taken too much human growth hormone

(HGH). Teddy was an army vet who had fought in Afghanistan. He was there because his girlfriend said she'd leave him if he didn't come.

Everyone already seemed exhausted.

Clark straightened up in his chair. "Now that we're all acquainted, I want to start off by letting you guys know what we're hoping to do here. Raphael and I are psychology students. After we heard that twenty percent of returning veterans suffer from PTSD, we saw the need for a local group like this.[5] Even though we've never had the honor of serving, we thought we might be able to help somehow ... and," he paused, as though he had something meaningful to say, "I want you all to know that although I never served in the military, I too have PTSD. In fact, anyone who experiences trauma, even growing up in a rough neighborhood, can develop—"

Jim, the one-armed vet, rolled his eyes.

"Excuse me," Jackson interrupted, brushing a long, grey hair from his face. "No offense, but I'm sick of hearing how everyone has PTSD. Suddenly, it's the new fad. Some kid is spanked by his parents, so he's got PTSD. Some black guy grows up on the wrong side of the tracks, he's got PTSD. Some white girl grows up on the wrong side of the tracks, she's got PTSD." He paused for a moment. "Cops, firefighters, and vets, they've all got *real* PTSD. Everyone else just has emotional baggage. I mean, this guy lost a fucking arm," he motioned toward Jim. Lou, the other Vietnam vet, nodded, along

---

5. The Department of Veterans Affairs, and various other veteran organizations, estimate that out of the 20 percent of Iraq and Afghanistan veterans with PTSD, less than half will seek treatment.

with both the Marines, Joe and Paul. All I could hear from Teddy was his slow, labored breathing.

Jim jumped in. "Real PTSD is when a veteran comes home from the war and is missing an arm! When he's kicked out of the military on medical! Has no job! And his wife leaves him!"

Just like that, the whole group was talking. I had figured it would've taken a few hours to get a room full of these guys talking, or at least a few beers. The Red Sox brothers insisted that Jim and Jackson were wrong, that anyone could get PTSD. The Marines Joe and Paul were with Jim and Jackson, and so was Lou, in thinking that vets had a monopoly on the thing. Gunner, Teddy, and I were the only ones not adding to the noise. Even Clark and Raphael had to raise their voices.

"Okay. Everyone please. Let's take things one at a time." Raphael's voice finally rose above the rest. "There will be plenty of time for discussion later."

Clark pulled his chair closer to the circle. "Well, first off, Teddy, why don't you join us?" He waved his arm forward. Everyone looked at Teddy, who didn't budge. After a few seconds, Clark continued, "All right, let's just start this thing. From now on, though, let's raise our hands if we have something to say."

Jackson raised his hand. "You didn't raise your hand to say that we should all raise our hands."

Jim laughed.

Clark shot Raphael a glance, and forced a smile. "Well, except for us, since we're running this thing. Okay?"

Raphael cleared his throat. "Okay. Let's start off with what post-traumatic stress disorder is and isn't." He picked up a clipboard from beneath his chair. "For today, we'll use the definition that post-traumatic stress disorder is an anxiety disorder that develops in people after they've been exposed to certain psychologically traumatic events. Does that make sense to everyone?"

Everyone nodded.

Raphael continued, mostly reading from his clipboard. "Symptoms manifest differently in different people. PTSD isn't a physical disease like chickenpox, where the signs and symptoms are similar for all people."

Lou walked over to the snack table, still sucking on his toothpick. He took it from his mouth to stick it into a piece of cheese.

Raphael and Clark seemed to be taking turns talking, serving the ball back and forth. "Some people have flashbacks, some people have nightmares, some just don't even know what they have and drown themselves in drugs or alcohol."

Somebody knocked on the door. Raphael got up to answer it. Pizza.

"Finally," Jackson huffed.

Clark stopped talking and shared a glance with Raphael. Clark stood. "Okay. I know we just began, but let's take a quick break. I think things will go smoother once we're all fed."

Everyone stood, except for Teddy, who just closed his eyes; pizza probably wasn't a good enough ratio of carbs to protein for him. Everyone else was in, though. Within a few minutes, cliques had formed. The Red Sox brothers were in one corner, the Marines Joe and Paul in another. The three Vietnam vets, Lou, Jackson, and

Jim, were standing next to the food table, and Gunner was talking with Clark and Raphael by their chairs. Teddy was still sitting with his eyes closed, and it was hard to tell if he was snoring or if it was his regular breathing. Then there was me. I poured some ginger ale.

I skipped the pizza and headed to the bathroom.

When I came back, the cliques were still intact; all that had changed was that Teddy's eyes were now open. He was leaning back in his chair, rocking. His feet were propped firmly on the ground, the chair resting on two legs as he inched forward and backward. He stared at me as I entered, and I felt like he knew what I'd just done. A week of sobriety. Gone. Here, of all places.

"Okay everyone," Clark announced. He was still standing there with Raphael and Gunner, in front of their chairs. "Let's take another five minutes, and then we'll get back at it."

Gunner glanced over his shoulder toward me, and put two fingers to his lips (the universal signal for a cigarette). I nodded, and we went outside. "What do you think?" I asked.

"Not what I expected," Gunner said in a tense whisper. "Not what I expected at all."

When we returned, I tried not to look at Teddy. It was silly of me to think he knew; I was just being paranoid. He should have kept his eyes closed, though. I felt Teddy looking at me as I spread butter across a cracker. Following me with his eyes as I poured another cup of ginger ale. Gunner had given me the rest of his Vicodin during the car ride, saying that he didn't need or want them anymore. But I did.

18

We sat back in a circle, now with our chairs turned around so that our backs were toward one another. Clark had just finished a fifteen-minute speech about stress and how it worsens the longer we hold it in. It was a boring, reading-from-a-clipboard lecture, and was made worse by constant interruptions from Jim and Jackson. But thankfully it was over. Clark now stood in the middle of our circle, where no one could see him, and he was telling us all to scream.

"Just scream," he said. He released a guttural yell. "Just like that."

The room went silent.

"Come on," Clark laughed. "I know it might sound weird, but give it a try."

Raphael, who was now seated next to me, let out a scream.

"Great, now who else wants to give it a a try?" Clark prodded.

"THIS IS STUPID!!" somebody screamed—probably Jackson, because Jim started laughing. I was sitting next to Raphael and Gunner, looking at the food table.

"All right. All right. Anyone else?" Clark asked once more.

We all sat there, waiting for someone to scream, expecting no one to. But then, to my surprise, Gunner did.

Right in my fucking ear. Louder than Clark and Raphael. And then he screamed again. He was going nuts. My ears were ringing.

Then, everyone else jumped in.

Everyone except for me. I still wasn't feeling it, and after a minute of the room sounding like an insane asylum, Clark told us that the screaming was just a warm-up. He had us in a circle with our backs to one another because he was going to ask us all questions, and he thought it would be easier if we weren't looking at one another. His first question was, "What was it like when you first returned home from the war?" He wanted us to talk about any memory that came to mind.

"When I got back," someone said, and the voice sounded gruff, like a smoker's. One of the Red Sox brothers, I assumed. "It was hard adjusting. I remember the first night home going to a bar with some friends—"

A few murmurs spread through the group.

"—but it just felt different. Like, I don't know … before I left, we had gone out for drinks, and then when I came home—and this was the same for both my deployments, but more for the second— but I just felt, like, like, like I wasn't home. Or, just, like, I wasn't sure about what was going on, or what I was supposed to do."

More murmurs of "mmhm" went through the group. One of these was from Gunner.

"That sounds about right," said someone else. Lou maybe, an older voice, and I imagined him speaking with the toothpick in his mouth. "Before you go to war, you're drinking with your buddies for fun, but afterwards you're still drinking, but your reasons have changed. This time it's to forget."

More murmurs of "mmhm," which was quickly becoming the pattern.

Raphael stirred next to me, and picked his clipboard off the ground. "What about Teddy, or Paul?" he asked, reading names from his board.

"Well," someone started speaking, "when I got back—"

Raphael cut them off. "Maybe it would help if we say our names."

"Good idea," Clark said, still standing in the middle of us all.

"I'm Paul," the same voice from a moment ago said, "and I just wanted to say that yeah, things were different coming home. Or *we* were different. But yeah, something had changed."

"How about this?" Raphael put his clipboard on the ground. "I think the conversation we want to have isn't going to come from scripted questions. What if you guys just talked to each other? Pretend we're not here. Share your stories and talk with a leaning toward your PTSD. Mike, how about you start us off?" He motioned toward me.

He'd asked at just the right moment—just as the Vicodin was

kicking in. I was feeling relaxed, almost giddy. "You know what I think?" I had a vague feeling that I wasn't on point with whatever question he'd asked, but I didn't care. "All those patriotic bumper stickers that say 'Never Forget,' with the backdrop of an American flag? They're all bullshit. The reality is that vets are always doing their best *to* forget—"

"Sing it, brother," someone said, which immediately made me regret sharing.

"Everything's different when you get back," someone else said, "even the things that are the same are different."

"No man ever steps in the same river twice, as Heraclitus put it."

"Things are just fucking *different*," someone jumped in.

"Yeah, *different*," said another.

And it seemed like no one could describe exactly what was *different*, only that it was the same for all of us.

"When I first got back," Jim was saying—he had the most distinctive voice: shrill and high pitched, almost like a young, angry boy. "First thing I did was go live in a tent out in the woods for two months. After everything that happened, I just needed to be alone. I didn't want to talk to or see anyone. And I still kinda feel that way."

Another of the Vietnam guys interjected—it sounded like Jackson. "First thing I did when I came home was punch one of those long-haired flowery guys in the face when he called me a murderer. I was just a boy. I went in towards the end. I didn't even kill anyone."

"Teddy. What about you?" asked Clark.

"When I came home, the first thing I did was head to the gym—"

Teddy said something else after "gym," but the laughter that came spewing out of my mouth drowned out whatever else he said. Gunner elbowed me to stop, which I did, just as Clark announced, "Let's move on to the next exercise." Raphael and Clark then had us arrange the chairs into groups of two—with the chairs facing each other. "Pick a random chair," Raphael announced after we'd finished, "and sit across from someone whom you don't know, or whom you didn't know before today."

Everyone slowly started moving for chairs. Jim sat across from Teddy, the Red Sox brothers sat across from Joe and Paul, and Gunner sat across from Jackson, which left me with toothpick Lou.

"For this exercise," Raphael was saying, "we want you to take turns with your partner. We want one of you to tell a story about the war, or coming home, and the other just needs to listen. The story can be made up or real, it doesn't matter. The only thing that has to happen is that the person talking has to talk for three minutes straight." Clark held up a stopwatch. "The other will hold eye contact and just listen, not saying anything. Then we'll switch."

I looked at Lou, still sucking away. He stared back, and I thought of my dating class with David and how the others had fallen asleep when we had to stare at one another. It felt so long ago. Another life. I couldn't believe it'd been almost three months.

"Ready? Begin."

Clark clicked his stopwatch.

"I'll go first," Lou said. "I guess I'll start at the beginning. The *real* beginning. I got no need to make anything up. I came home after thirteen months over there." He looked into my eyes as though he was trying to be deep, and he continued sucking on his toothpick, like he was an old cowboy. Even though I was on Vicodin, he was getting on my nerves. "I killed over there, had friends die… lots of friends. When I came home, half my high school class was either dead or over there—" He stopped his story, leaned toward me. "You ever seen someone die?" he asked. He suckled loudly on his toothpick, spittle on the sides of his lips, and his eyes peered into mine, searching for my answer. I stared back, giving away nothing.

He was doing a veteran's proverbial dick measuring. How much combat had you seen? How many dead bodies? Confirmed kills? Even though you may have been to war, been through hell, missed your family, come close to death, saved hundreds of lives, had people die in your hands, you could still somehow have done something more or seen more. Someone always had it worse. Someone had always done more. Enough was never enough. That's how it was for all of us. The only unimpeachable ones were the ones who died. And even though I may not have killed anyone, or been in direct firefights, working in the hospital, we all saw more blood, and had more people dead and dying in our hands daily, than most people did over their entire deployments. I mentioned none of it to Lou, though. Because screw his scorekeeping.

We continued for a few more moments, and I wished I had the power to put him to sleep, but Lou was too stubborn. He shook his head, as though whatever suspicions he had about me were correct, and continued talking.

"Time's up," Clark said a minute later. "Take a breather and we'll go again in a minute."

"Hey, before I begin," I was still staring at Lou. "Do you mind taking the toothpick out of your mouth?"

His eyes narrowed. He looked disgusted. "Excuse me?"

"Can you take the toothpick out of your mouth?"

"What does it matter, son?"

"Yeah, exactly. What *does* it matter?"

He didn't respond, but his silence spoke for itself.

His lips puckered, like he'd just sucked on a lemon, and he took out the toothpick. He placed it behind his ear, and then it promptly fell to the ground. I couldn't have planned it better.

"Ready. Begin!" hollered Clark. He and Raphael sauntered around the room, listening here and there to the conversations. Most of which, I assumed, were similar. War was only about one thing, after all. Clark stopped near me and Lou. He listened to me share some bullshit story from my deployment, something that meant nothing, that shared nothing of myself. "Okay. Time's up!" he shouted next to my ear.

Clark and Raphael then gave another lecture, this time about "stress-coping mechanisms," which was really just them spending ten minutes telling us to take deep breaths and to "count to ten" when feeling stressed. Pretty soon, the meeting was ending and Clark was talking. "If you start getting bad thoughts, just think about something else," he was saying.

A chorus of laughter came from one-armed Jim, Lou, and Jackson.

"Why didn't I think of that?" Jackson joked.

Jim laughed harder, slapping his knee as though it was the funniest thing ever. This clearly egged Jackson on.

"Seriously. It's genius," Jackson proclaimed. "Problem solved."

Raphael rubbed his palms against his thighs, as though he was smoothing out wrinkles. Jackson was clearly pissing him off. "Okay. Okay. I know some things are easier said than done—"

"No shit!" Jackson interrupted, which caused Jim to start laughing again.

My gaze drifted from Gunner to Clark and Raphael, to Teddy and toothpick Lou, and then back to Gunner. I couldn't get out of there fast enough. Clark and Raphael passed around a sheet for us to add our e-mail addresses, and after writing down a fake one, Gunner and I were out of there. Neither one of us even bothered to say goodbye.

"That was bullshit, man," Gunner said as he started his car. He revved the engine. "I mean, what the hell were we even doing in there? And how the fuck was any of that supposed to help me?" He raised his eyebrows, and actually was suppressing tears.

I heard the frustration in his voice. I could feel it in myself, too. Two hours ago, when we first arrived, I thought this group was going to be stupid. Now I knew I was right.

"I know," I told him.

"You know, on the bridge…" he peeled out of the parking lot, white knuckling the steering wheel. "You know, I was ready, man.

I was ready to fucking do it." The last part of the sentence was spoken so quietly that I almost couldn't understand him. He started breathing deeper, driving faster.

"I know, man."

"Yeah—"

"I've been there—"

"No, you haven't!" he snapped.

A vague feeling of nausea fluttered in my stomach. I breathed in, holding it for a few seconds, hoping it'd calm me down. I exhaled.

"I haven't been there?!"

My heart pounded. I looked at him from the corner of my eye. Gunner suddenly looked so small.

A tear strolled down his cheek. "It's fucking hopeless," he said.

19

At first I couldn't believe what she was wearing. A black-and-white dress, *painted on*, which ended just below her waist. It was the type of dress that made women jealous. And she seemed to embrace that possibility.

"What are you looking at?" she smirked.

Her name was Lisa. She was thirty years old, a "trophy wife" (her description), and the two of us were outside smoking while our drug-abuse meeting was on break. Natalie had suggested I go to the meeting. I wanted to be at this thing even less than I had wanted to be at the PTSD group, but I figured I'd give it a shot. Nothing else seemed to be working.

Everything looked exactly as you'd expect at this place. Exactly like it looked for the PTSD meeting. Different church and different people, sure, but the same uncomfortable chairs, same cheese and crackers, the same feeling.

In ten minutes, we'd have to go back inside and listen to more people bitch about their lives. Financial problems seemed to be the biggest concern—and not in the way you'd think. The meeting took place in a wealthy suburb of Boston, and most of the people were there because they had too much money. Lisa explained what I was in for; this was a group full of trophy wives like her. They were bored with their husbands, bored with their lives. Most of the older women were addicted either to weight-loss pills they were given by their personal trainers, or pain-killers they were given by their doctors. The younger women (Lisa indicated herself at this point) were guilty of a higher-energy high. She was here for ecstasy.

She handed me her pack as she walked in to use the bathroom—I'd bummed my earlier one from her. "Knock yourself out," she said.

"Thanks," I replied.

I smoked another, and then tried to stay for the rest of the meeting, but halfway through hearing another story about getting a boob job and then becoming addicted to Vicodin, I walked out.

In twenty minutes I was at Pete's Bar & Grille, an island themed bar that often had live music and, in the warmer months, an outdoor area with a sand floor. It was a casual place, albeit a little too close to where I went to high school. I wasn't in the mood to run into anyone. I was just killing time and drinking until I was supposed to be done with the meeting and could go see Natalie. The group had been a waste of time, like I was saying to the bartender. But in a way, I was jealous. They all seemed to know why they were popping pills. Boredom. Body image. Bad advice. But for me? After all these months, I still had no idea what made me feel so empty and kept me using whatever was on hand. The memories? My derelict, corrupt commanders? The dead? The near-death experiences? The war itself? If I just knew the culprit, I thought, maybe I could do something. Make peace with it. But I didn't know. I didn't know what had fucked me up. And I think that's what fucked me up the most.

I looked around the bar. College kids from Bridgewater State were horsing around, and sorority girls were looking for attention. There were some older women there, too, in groups, laughing too loudly. One of them, Brenda, walked over to me, ready to pounce. A few minutes later, with another beer for both of us, we started talking about the war. It was all I ever talked about, I knew it. For a long time, I thought I spent so much time talking about the war because everyone else kept bringing it up, but recently I'd begun to realize that it was my fault. I was the one constantly bringing it up. I'd become *that guy*. I might as well have been wearing my dog tags on the outside of my shirt. I was my own worst enemy, and there was nothing I could do about it.

Brenda, worn down from a hard day of work, or from the kids, ex-husband, or something, told me, "My son said he's joining the military. He's only seventeen!"

"You Shook Me All Night Long" played on the radio. I tapped a pack of cigs on the bar to the beat. I didn't know how she wanted me to respond.

"Can you believe that?" she asked. "How old were you when

you joined?"

"Seventeen."

"Oh…"

I was feeling pretty good, getting drunk and listening to her. The only problem was that I couldn't smoke indoors. I took a cigarette out of the pack, and put it behind my ear for later. Went back to tapping to the beat.

"I was reading about the soldiers over there in the paper today," she said.

A crowd of people entered the bar. More college kids. She started raising her voice. "Crazy stuff over there. I think President Bush and the generals need to change strategies, because it doesn't look like the surge is—"

"What do you know about it?"

Her eyes clicked open and shut. A confused shake of her head. "Excuse me?"

My phone vibrated. Gunner, of course. He was having a cookout tomorrow—in the dead of fucking winter—and wanted me to be there. "Its importnt that u cum." The accidental obscenity of text messaging.

"What's the problem? We're all Americans here," she was saying. "I can see when things are going wrong. They need to send even more troops in there to fight the terrorists. And it's not just *your* war; it's America's war."

But it was "our war," and always would be. It may be the politicians and talking heads who sent us there, and it may be public sentiment that kept us there, but none of them should mistake this, or any war, for theirs. War always has belonged, and always will belong, to those who put themselves on the line. Nobody else seemed to understand that. And I knew I shouldn't hold it against this woman. But, sometimes, civilian thoughts and military actions just get muddled.

"You've got no idea what you're talking about," I told her.

"Excuse me?"

"You shouldn't talk about something you know nothing about."

"I'm entitled to an opinion."

"No, you're not. You're not entitled to shit. And what you're spouting off isn't just an opinion. It's bullshit."

"Where do you get off—?"

"Just forget it, okay?"

"I support the troops—"

My voice was loud, I realized, and it was getting louder the more I spoke. "You what? Have a bumper sticker on your fucking car?"

It was almost a full-blown argument now, but luckily, the bar was loud enough that no one was paying any attention. AC/DC was over, and now some pop-music crap was playing. Not that we could really hear the music anymore. She opened her purse, grabbed her wallet, and it looked like she was getting ready to pay. I could see that she was upset.

"Listen… I've had a few—" I looked at her as earnestly as I could. "No need to leave on my account. I'm sorry."

I waited for her to respond.

She sat back down, ordered another drink, and stopped fidgeting with her purse. "So what is it that the troops *need* then?"

"I don't know. I'm not the one to ask."

Someone tapped me on the shoulder.

Here we go, I thought. I turned around, expecting to see a drunken friend of hers. But what I saw instead was short, spikey hair and a smiling, familiar face. I nearly stumbled out of my stool.

"Jesus Christ! Sellers! How you been?"

I went to give her a hug, but she backed up. Her expression changed to one of alarm. *What's that all about?* I thought sourly, but then another thought quickly hit me, and I laughed in relief. *How could I forget! Germs!* Sellers was the germaphobe. The one who inspired me to wash my hands *before* going to the bathroom. To build a nest on every public toilet. She taught me never to share drinks with a stranger, or even a friend. And never to hug anyone. *Ever.* We bumped fists.

Her eyes smiled back, embracing me from a safe distance. "I've been good. How about you?"

"Meh." I took a sip of beer. "Been better. But good."

Brenda stood up, tossed me a sideward glance, and said, "It was nice meeting you," as she walked off.

"What are you doing here?" I had one of those stupid drunken grins on my face. I knew it. My jaw was already starting to hurt.

"I'm here visiting friends."

"Wow. I never thought I'd see you again."

"I know. It's good to see you out of uniform. I always wondered what you'd look like as a civilian."

There were more than a few reasons I was excited to see Sellers.

The first was that I never thought I'd see her again. The second had to do with her dream of owning a bar. When you're in a war zone, you tell yourself that when you come home, you're going to do something big. Something to make going to war worthwhile. Sellers and another friend, Denti, had talked about opening a bar together. We all knew it was never really going to happen, though. Everyone just needed a story to tell themselves to get through the deployment. I had told myself I was going to become a writer. Another friend was going to become a doctor; someone else was going to move to Hollywood and become an actor. What we'd do when we returned home got us through the war, even if they were just fantasies. I hoped that at least one of us would follow through.

Because we were both drunk, the conversation that followed was easy and natural.

"Seen any good movies?"

"Any funny stories since coming home?"

"Run into anyone else?"

Overall, she said she was doing well, and that she'd gotten better about dealing with her germaphobia, but I doubted it. Not only was there the whole hug thing, but whenever some drunken college kid was moving past her, she tried to give them as much space as possible, so that not even a shred of clothing brushed up against her.

Then things got a little heavier.

"How you handling being back?"

"Still taking Ambien?"

"Been hitting the bottle?"

We answered honestly. I did, anyway. And we talked for a few more minutes—turns out she had given up on her dream of owning a bar (too much paperwork, too little money)—and even though we were both smiling and excited to see one another, she looked as though she was struggling with things, too. In Iraq, she had been a hard worker, an honest person. One of the best soldiers in the unit, actually. Which is why it wasn't surprising that she would be having trouble coming home. As every retention officer tells outgoing troops, "Good soldiers make bad civilians." An insomniac like her—who would work twenty hours a day, seven days a week—someone like her couldn't just go home. The blood of war doesn't come off with soap. It stains.

"I've been seeing this girl for a while," I told her.

"Is it serious?"

I shrugged. "I'm not sure I'm ready for something serious." Which was a bit of an understatement, given my state of mind and how meaningless things had been feeling. I told her I wasn't sure if I was ready for anything at all.

She nodded.

Gunner was texting again.

"I'm seeing someone too," Sellers said.

The vague use of "someone" kept up the suspense that had been building on the topic of Sellers' sexuality for almost as long as I'd known her. In Iraq, entertainment was hard to come by. A man could only reread the same *Reader's Digest* so many times before he needed something else to distract him. The affairs of our fellow soldiers were enough to keep us all from blowing our heads off.

Who was sleeping with whom? Who was cheating the government out of money? Who was the one who stole the night-vision goggles? Was Sellers into men or women? It wasn't that anyone cared in *that* sense—we were a liberal reserve unit from Massachusetts, after all—but everyone was curious. We *had* to know! And plus, she was good looking, so everyone was interested.

She motioned to someone behind her, someone who must've been there the whole time while we were talking.

I extended a hand. "Hi. I'm Michael."

A hand shot back at me. "Hi. Nice to meet you." Then the person looked at Sellers. "I'll let you two keep talking. I'll grab a drink over here."

The mystery was solved, not that I actually cared.

"That's all right," I told Sellers and her friend. "I was getting ready to go." I chugged the last of my beer, threw a twenty on the bar. "Hey, it was good seeing you again."

"Yeah. You too."

"Let's try and keep in touch."

"Yeah. Definitely."

We both knew it was a lie; neither of us were the type to keep in touch, but it was a hopeful lie. The kind we wished might be true.

20

After a dozen additional text messages from Gunner, including one at five in the morning, I knew there was no way I could skip his cookout. Natalie and Wilson had to work, so I drove an hour and a half to suburban Boston to see him. Gunner's father rented him the bottom floor of a light-brown, three-family house with vinyl siding and dark brown shutters. I had to park a half a mile away because the narrow street he lived on was already crowded with cars. When I finally reached the apartment, Gunner's front door was wide open. I poked my head in.

"Hello!" I called out.

No one was there.

An eerie feeling shot through me, but then I saw Gunner out back on his deck. He was clearly drunk, grilling and singing "Down on the Corner" along with Credence Clearwater—but flat and off key, in his case. He also happened to have zero rhythm. The sun was just setting, and I could see clouds rolling in. I walked in but stopped short, half in the house and half on the deck. I'd been here once before, and things were different. His TV was nowhere in sight, his couch was gone, and his dining-room table was missing all its chairs.

I interrupted his singing. "Hey. Gunner."

He turned around. "Yo! Mikey!" He was way too excited to see me. "What's up, man?! What are you doing here?"

"Um … you invited me over for a—"

"Oh. Right. Right." He turned back around and flipped a burger on the grill. "Sorry, no plates and no buns. We'll have to eat with our hands. Like we're back in the army!" Gunner shivered as he spoke. It was freezing outside, and he was wearing only boxer shorts, sandals, and a tank top.

"Is everything all right?" I asked. "Where's all your furniture?"

"Just making a change, man. Getting rid of all the junk in my life."

Normally, I wouldn't have bothered prying. It's hard to care when you're suicidal. But he was acting too weird for me to just let it go.

"Are you sure—"

"Yeah. Yeah. I'm totally fine. You need a beer." He walked over to his cooler on the other side of his deck, grabbed two Coronas, and handed me one.

After walking back toward the grill, he slid the spatula underneath the burger and held it up to my face. "Take it," he urged. "It's yours, man."

The offer was sweet, considering that it was the only hamburger on the grill. However, there were no plates or napkins, so I just told him I had to take a piss. Once inside, I threw some cold water on my face, took a minute, and then headed back out to the deck.

He was waiting for me right outside the bathroom.

"You know what I was thinking—"

"Jesus Christ, man!" I yelled, startled. "Give me some fucking space."

"Oh, sorry. Anyways … you know what I was thinking?"

I had absolutely no idea. I told him as much, and he laughed as we made our way into the living room. Then he became serious, pacing the room, his arms flapping. "I saw on the news that they're thinking of sending in more troops. It's, like, *wasteful*, when you think about it … like, what's the point?"

I leaned against the spot on the wall where his flat-screen TV used to be. It was all he talked about last time I had been there. Plasma, high-def, and picture in picture, but now all that remained were two holes in the wall. Even the drywall screws were gone.

He went through all the reasons that people fought wars: honor, duty, family, friends, revenge, money, power, liberty, and freedom. He listed reasons why he thought they were all bullshit. Even the righteous reasons were bullshit, he said. Now wasn't the time for debate about his new anti-war stance.

"Listen," he said breathlessly. "We killed a lot of insurgents over there… and I don't, like, regret it… I had to… but I don't…" He cleared his throat and then repeated himself. "We *had* to… b-but…

I don't li-like being called a hero because of it. You know?"

The army had trained us to be heroes, as though it were possible to train for such a thing. But no real hero sees himself as one, and therein lay the catch-22. No good soldier or righteous person is called a hero and agrees with it. He merely nods his head—"I was just doing my job, Ma'am"—and is done with it. What ordinary people would consider "heroic" in regular life is often just a typical day for a soldier at war. Thus, no good soldier sees himself as an individual hero. There are other soldiers, though, a small subset known as the "hero-grabbers." They latch onto the designation. They tell stories to anyone who will listen. These guys just do it to sound cool, or be called the "hero." Those who really experienced the horror of war tend to talk about it differently. They tell jokes, or say nothing at all, because the other stories are too hard to tell, too pointless, too personal.

I looked at the two trees in Gunner's backyard, fighting against the cold, hard wind. I watched the trees shaking and dancing in the shade. The problem, I was thinking, is that when fighting and killing become your ordinary existence, and then you're home and sitting around watching TV and working some meaningless job, that's when the depression hits. That's when guys start volunteering for multiple deployments. That's when—

Gunner was obsessively pacing in his underwear in front of me. He began biting his fingers. Gnawing at the edges, spitting skin and nail onto the ground.

"Are you all right?" he asked.

"Yeah. Wait, what?" I nodded, somewhat taken aback. He was

the one who needed help here, not *me*.

There was a long silence.

The door to his deck was still open. A breeze swept through the room. Gunner mumbled something, and then I heard him say Natalie's name.

"What was that?" I asked.

"The Illuminati should—"

"No. You mentioned Natalie."

"How're things between you two?"

"They're—"

"You know, man," he interrupted. "Treat her right. If I had a girl like that, I'd treat her right. Get her flowers every day. Call her every day. Say nice things to her. I'd even get her mom to like me. That's important, you know. To get a girl's mom to like you. That would change everything. Getting a nice girlfriend... you know, I was dating a new girl... you would've liked her." He stopped chewing on his fingers and looked around. He seemed scared, almost paranoid.

He shook his head, sighed, and rubbed at his brow. "She was a cool girl," he was babbling. "Probably dating some jerk now..."

"I'm sure you can find—"

"She was beautiful, too—"

"Come on, man. There's plenty of fish in the—"

Everything in my life has been boiled down to two things: war and women. It seemed the same for Gunner.

"We went on a few dates," he said, staring at an unknown point on the wall. "Then, I don't know... we were having sex and I asked her to choke me a little. Not with a rope or anything, just her hands, you know… and then she just up and *left*. She, like, broke up with me right in the middle of—"

I interrupted. "Sounds pretty typical to me," I joked.

"That's funny," he said with a straight face.

"Thanks."

He took a step backward, his face lightening. "No, seriously. I've always enjoyed your sense of humor."

"Thanks. Me too."

"That's why I want you to have my dining-room table," he motioned toward the table with his hand. "It has everything except the chairs."

"Um… What?"

"Yeah, take it, man. It's quality stuff."

"No thanks."

"You sure?"

"Yup."

He reached into his pocket, and took something out. "What if I threw in these?" He held up a metallic pair of nail clippers. They looked like the ones he had taken from my house a few weeks earlier.

"Wait a second… aren't those—"

"Actually, forget it." He turned around, and put the clippers back in his pocket. "I promised the table to my friend Jerry." He walked back out on his deck. "Want another beer?"

What I was realizing, as Gunner stumbled around the apartment, was that war isn't what breaks a soldier. It isn't being a trained killer, and killing, nor is it the constant brushes with death and the loss of fellow soldiers. What actually breaks a soldier isn't the fighting and dying. It's the peace. That's what kills us. A veteran is more than *fifty* times more likely to kill themselves at home, at peace, than at war. That should be the answer to everyone who thinks that war breaks soldiers. War isn't what does it. Coming home is.

Holding two beers in my hand—the one from earlier that I was still drinking, and the one Gunner just handed me—I told him that maybe we should call someone. Maybe a family member or friend he could talk to. Someone, anyone, besides me.

"Why man? I feel great. Better than ever!"

"You don't look so good."

"Neither do you, man. Maybe we should call someone for *you*—"

"Look, man. *I'm* fine."

"Well, me too! I feel great! What do you want me to do? Run around the block? I'll do it." He headed for his bedroom. "I think I have running shoes somewhere around here."

We stood in his bedroom as he put on his sneakers. His hands shook as he bent over and tied the laces. As soon as he finished, he giggled, and then kicked off the shoes again. "I'm not going running," he laughed. "That's crazy." He jumped on his bed and crawled beneath the covers. He told me he was tired and that I should let myself out.

21

Bad weather, all winter. Natalie and I sat indoors all weekend and drank all night.

"When you talk about the military, it seems," she said, "…to have a certain poetry to—"

"I don't think so…"

"I think we learn that, Michael—will you let me finish?"

"Doing guard duty with the Ugandans, hearing their chants and stories—maybe that's poetry."

"Fine."

"Clutching your knees in bunkers for hours as mortars drop—"

"Forget it."

"Listening to the alarms of 'all clear' ring throughout—"

"Okay. I'm sorry."

"Blood gushing and squirting from bullet and shrapnel

wounds. Women and children and soldiers and terrorists screaming—"

"I just think if you can let me finish what I was saying—"

"Help. Help! Help!! There's rhythm there, at least. Gush, squirt,
scream. Gush, squirt, scream! Gush! Squirt! Scream!"

"Okay! Just forget it!"

A grenade is thrown into an encampment. A soldier jumps on
it to save his friends. That's the poetry of war. But poetry's supposed
to be beautiful, too. What's the beauty of a dead soldier? The poetry
of a man willing to die? And how was I supposed to explain to her
that it all left me feeling empty?

"You need to see Gunner and Wilson."

"This fucking weather…"

"My father wants me to temp at a law firm during winter
break."

"Fine."

"Take me somewhere. Get me out of this house—"

So we started going to the dog track. Natalie had never been, not
that she was missing much: grungy chairs, peanut shells, and losing
tickets littering the ground. Gamblers and drunks—addicts either
way—all congregated together amidst the smell of mustard and beer.
But it was something different, and getting out of the house put us
both in better moods. We became regulars for a few days. One night,
I was sitting at a table near a large window, facing the track, munch-
ing on French fries and drinking a Bud Light. She ran over as soon as
she saw me, still in work clothes: a blue silk blouse, long plaid skirt,
nylons, and high heels. She looked sexy as hell.

"Hey, how was work?"

"It was... uh... it's over?"

She fell onto my lap and I squeezed her tight. Too tight, apparently.

"Oww! Lighter next time. I'm not one of your army buddies."

"You think I hug Gunner like that?"

She kissed me.

"You want a beer or something?"

"Sure."

I held up my brew and two fingers toward the closest waitress. "Two more please," I mouthed.

"S-so..." Natalie started saying, as I ordered, which I knew meant bad news. She always stammered when she was nervous.

"What is it?"

"I think we should talk. About... things." She got up, and sat across from me at the table. "I think the relationship needs to be... exclusive."

"Okay? Why now?"

"Because I see a serious future for us."

The waitress came with our drinks.

"So... what do you think?" Natalie prodded.

"I—I... I don't know—"

"What? You don't know what?"

"We're having fun here, why—"

She sighed. "Alright. Nevermind. Let's talk about something else." She looked away, took a sip of her drink, rubbed the label with her thumb. It took about another sixty seconds of silence for her to change the subject.

"I think you should see one of my dad's friends."

"What kind of friend?"

"He's a psychiatrist with a military background."

"I don't think—"

"This would help you—"

The races began. The speaker in the background started announcing the dogs. "Little Man takes the lead! Starlight is right behind and in the rear is…"

"It doesn't even seem worth it. You don't have to stay with me, you know."

"Dragon Quest is still in the lead but it looks like Little Man is getting his second wind…"

"Michael—"

"I don't even understand it. I really don't. Why do you want to be with me? Is it because I'm some fucked-up vet?"

"What? Why would you even ask me that?"

"Do you want to fix me?"

"No!"

"I just don't understand it. That's all."

"Just tell me what you need."

"I don't know. I don't know what I need. I just need a cigarette, that's all."

"You know I'm here for you. I can help!"

"Yeah. *I know.* Thanks."

"And it looks like… YES! … Little Man is going to take the race after all… and YES… he has it!"

We went outside. I lit a cigarette. Underneath the awning, a dozen other smokers stood around, a cool breeze blowing and moisture in the air. Natalie asked me again to see her dad's friend.

"Do it for me," she said.

She took a deep breath and looked into my eyes. She was about to say something big. She held my hand, giving it a gentle squeeze. I returned the gesture and thought how strange it was that our hands could hold our emotions. Sadness. Anxiety. Fear. From a trembling hand, to a clenched fist, to a sweaty palm.

"It's just that, you know... I—I love you."

Humans are lucky though, that we can rely on so many different types of communication. Words, hands, expressions, intonation, and the rest of the unconscious gesticulations that we make. It all *speaks*. Her hands said nothing. But her smile, the way her voice rose and intoned a sense of caring when she said, "I love you," it told me everything I needed to know. She truly believed what she was saying; she was in fucking love.

I took a breath. I didn't feel the same way. Or, at least, I didn't think so. "I don't know how I feel about things. I'm working through some shit."

"Just tell me what you need, Michael."

"I don't know," I said. "I don't know what I need."

22

As I listened to Commando on the phone, all I could think about was Scout, my brother's German Shepard. One day, when I was a kid, we were having a cookout when he jumped on my back and knocked the wind out of me. It was the first time I remembered struggling to breathe. I felt the same way now as Commando talked, each breath filled with confusion, even panic. He asked a question, but I couldn't respond. I gripped the desk in front of me to stop my hands from shaking.

"You still there?" he asked.

I had been falling asleep when he called, but now I was wide awake. "Um… yeah. I'm here." I grabbed a pack of cigarettes and ripped it open, but everything was crushed. Shreds of tobacco poured from the pack into my hands.

"You all right, man?" he asked.

"Um… yeah… yeah. Thanks for letting me kno—"

"And hey, listen," he interrupted, "now might not be the best time, but if you're ever back in Boston, let's meet up and hit on some—"

I hung up.

Natalie leaned over in bed. "Who was that?"

I pretended I hadn't heard. She had come back again.

"You look pale… everything okay?"

It was a little past midnight and Commando just told me some miserable news. Gunner was in the hospital. He had tried to kill himself. So, no, I wasn't okay. I turned face down in my bed, and cupped a pillow between my ears. If I could just block it all out. I never thought that he would actually try.

Late at night, after spending all day drinking in his unfurnished apartment, Gunner downed a handful of Ambien, took a razor, and slit one of his wrists. He passed out before he had a chance to slit the other, and that's when his brother found him lying face down on the cold linoleum of his bathroom, his arms limp at his sides, one of his wrists flayed open, and blood pooled everywhere. Gunner's brother took him to the hospital. The next day, his brother went back and cleaned up the dried blood—the "suicide grease," as Commando had described it. I couldn't *not* think of it. It was a bad scene, Commando had said. The reason he had found out was because he had gone to high school with Gunner's brother. Who knows how long it would've taken for us to find out otherwise?

I couldn't get the image out of my head: Gunner's thick, PTSD-laced blood dripping from his wrist. His face growing pale, his body turning cold. His blood infected with his misery. Anyone coming in contact with PTSD gets the disease; PTSD acts like a disease, that's what I think. One article I'd read said that a single person suffering from PTSD could "infect" the people around him with similar symptoms. A father could pass the symptoms to his kids. A husband to his wife. Wife to kids. It was endless, inevitable. Gunner's blood was wreaking havoc on his family, just like mine would do to my own, or would have.

"Michael. What is it?" Natalie lifted the pillow over my head. I had no idea how long she'd been asking the question, but I wanted to be alone.

"What's going on?" she asked again.

"It's nothing."

"It's not nothing. What is it?"

She just wouldn't let it drop. Question after question, until I had an outburst.

"You want to fucking know? Gunner tried to kill himself."

"… Michael, I didn't—"

"Okay? You happy now?"

"No, of course—"

I pressed the pillow against my ears, and could feel the blood pounding through my veins. What could I have done? My mind wandered, as I looked for pieces of the puzzle. I replayed scenes from the cookout. Giving away his furniture. Acting erratic. The confusion. The forgetfulness. I knew something was way off. I should've done something. It was Crade all over again. Images of Gunner putting on his running shoes and then crawling into bed played on repeat.

I felt Natalie's legs brush against me in the darkness, then the springs squeaked and the bed lightened. She was going somewhere. I could hear her getting dressed. Then there was the sound of her footsteps as she crept down the stairs. She was leaving. I thought about getting out of the house myself. But I had no clue where to go.

My feet sounded louder than Natalie's as I walked down the stairs and into the kitchen. I heard a toilet flush as I walked to the front door. She hadn't gone anywhere yet. The bathroom door squeaked open as I closed the front one. I could feel Natalie peering out the kitchen window at me as I got in my car. The engine roared, the tires peeled, and dirt kicked up as I pulled away down the road. I just needed to think.

The evening clouds floated lazily in the sky, the sun was making its way toward evening, and the husbands and wives who'd gotten out of work late were just then pulling into their driveways. It would've been quite the idyllic scene, if not for me and Gunner. I was holding him by his shirt collar.

"What the hell, man," I shouted angrily.

How could you do this?

From the edge of his driveway where I now stood, I could see people starting to stare. The old woman across the street walking her dog, the little boy checking the mail for his mother, the two other little boys tossing snow at one another, and a man getting out of his car. They all looked over, but none of them knew. No one knew. Gunner's phone had been shut off, so finding out information was an onerous task. I'd had to call Commando, who would then call Gunner's brother, and then call me back. Then repeat the next day, as new information came forward. Gunner was in the hospital. He was doing well. He was coming home. Somewhere in all that, Natalie was constantly calling. I hadn't talked to her since I'd found out about Gunner five days earlier. She wouldn't stop calling, pestering, annoying the hell out of me. Any thought I had of the two of us staying together was so gone.

"I'm sorry, man," Gunner said. The words came out slowly and he choked up. "It was a dumb thing to do."

A decorated soldier, a hero, and now, he'd be labeled a mental case. A nut job. The flags, handshakes, and bumper stickers. They were for him, and this was the price he paid.

"I'd stopped taking the meds." By the calm, focused look in his eyes, I knew he meant it. "A friend was hurt in a firefight overseas—"

"It's okay." I let go of his shirt collar. "It's okay, man," I said again.

"You're pissed, huh?" he asked. And for a moment, the focused, clear-minded look in his eyes was replaced by a deadened stare.

"No. I mean, I don't know." My eyes strained to avoid his. I stared back out across the street. The boy had brought the mail inside to his mother. The man had gone into his house. The woman with her dog was gone. The two boys who were playing in the snow were probably inside by now. We were the same, though.

"So listen," he began. "I'm going to Texas to live with my sister and … I don't know when I'll be back up here." And as he said, "up here," there was a silence between us, an unbreakable, unbreachable wall. Thinking about it, I had really only known Gunner a few weeks. Meetings at bars, driving around, the PTSD group, a late night on the bridge—that was about it. It was a whirlwind, one-night-stand kind of friendship. "But it's been good knowing you, man." He extended his hand.

I breathed as deeply as possible, and felt the fading sun on my skin. There was a sense of fear and hopefulness in his voice, as though the worst and best were both on the horizon.

The embrace was short. As we backed up, Gunner told me to say "bye" to Natalie for him.

"Sure, yeah, of course."

"Later, man." Gunner walked back inside his house. I got into my car and drove away. I stared out the window and watched the trees and houses and other cars as I passed by.

Well, at least there's always Wilson. God help us.

23

Four Marlboro Reds, one Red Bull, three beers, a bit of tequila, and half a Vicodin. I was alone in my bedroom, flipping through my journal, looking at the entries I'd written since returning home. I began to see a pattern. I realized that my emotions weren't, or hadn't been, turned off as much as I thought, or had hoped. They were still there, in a way, but just different than they'd been before the war. Like a bike left out in the rain, parts were rusted, and just didn't spin like they used to. I looked back at my writings about David, Wilson, Gunner, Samantha, and Natalie. The entries were more upbeat than I would have thought. They seemed almost hopeful, and for a few days after meeting Natalie, you wouldn't have even been able to tell what I really had in mind.

But there were the dark parts, too. The fights in San Diego. The suicide line. The homeless veteran. Gunner's night on the bridge.

Not to mention the dozens of incoherent ramblings, which I knew meant that I was stoned as hell. And then there were all the times I had been a complete ass to Natalie. I still had no idea why she was with me. She deserved better. At the very least, she deserved a break from me.

I'd planned on breaking things off at Olive Garden. It would be my first official breakup, and taking my cue from TV shows, a restaurant seemed like the best place. We'd meet. Enjoy a nice meal. Have a casual conversation. Break up. And then say goodnight. Simple.

Or so I had hoped. But when I told Natalie that I'd meet her there, she was confused, as I had always picked her up before. So to her it had seemed odd that I now wanted her to meet me in a separate car.

The plan went downhill from there. When I couldn't come up with a good reason for meeting her there, I wound up just picking her up at her house again, which made everything more difficult. I couldn't break up with her in a restaurant, and then spend thirty minutes driving back to her place. The new plan was to break up with her on the way home, right as I was dropping her off. I just had to get through the meal.

We were sitting across from one another. Our table was covered in plates, covered in half-eaten food, and we were making small talk. The whole dinner had been small talk. Since I was preparing to break up with her, it felt like a lie to bring the conversation any deeper than the weather, TV, and how much to tip our waiter. Chit chat.

"You ready to go?"

She nodded.

We stood. I grabbed my drink, finished the last few drops, and threw some money on the table—and then some more, after a look from Natalie.

When we got out the door, she surprised me again. "Give me your car keys."

"What? Why?"

"You're too drunk to drive."

A minute later, I was in the passenger seat. My palms were sweating and I was mumbling something about relationships, and people, and how it related to *us*.

"Things can never work out in a relationship where one person is more fucked up than the other," I explained. "For a relationship to work, two people have to be similarly fucked up. If there's any difference in the level of fucked-up-edness, then one person is always going to be trying to change the other one. And that fuckin' sucks."

She'd stopped listening.

She was shaking her head back and forth, repeating, "I don't get it… what does this have to do with us?"

I looked over at her face, sweet and confused. She smiled and turned away. I didn't know what else to do; all that was left was the brutal truth.

"Oh. Before I forget," she said before I had a chance. "I was reading this story in the newspaper about someone you might know."

I was thankful for the distraction, not sure if I could've handled the honest route. "Really? Who?" I asked excitedly.

"It was about this guy who had recently returned from Iraq. He worked in a hospital, too, and the article was about how hard it was over there and how this guy was, like, this great leader and hero and—"

"What's his name?"

"I think the article was about a Colonel... Lolllydash or something—"

"Pull over."

"What?"

"Natalie! Pull the fucking car over!"

My heart thudded, pounded, in my throat. Something cold griped me. I couldn't breathe. Natalie pulled the car over and I could hear her asking if I was all right and what was going on. I kept trying harder to breathe, to focus.

"Michael, what's wrong?" she asked.

"Do you know him?" she asked.

"Should I start driving again?" she asked.

"Are you okay?" she asked.

I flicked my lighter on and off, on and off, not because I was getting ready to smoke. Colonel Lollydash was the big-nosed, big-mouthed, and big-bellied colonel who was awarded a Bronze Star for "heroism." But he was anything but a hero. I flicked the lighter on once more, and this time lit a cigarette. Natalie had pulled off near a wooded area, and I stared at the trees as I smoked.

Taking long drags, studying the tree closest to me, I sat there for a few seconds in rigid silence. "Tell me everything about this article," I finally said, after exhaling a stream of smoke.

"I don't know … It was in the local paper, about that Lollydash guy and how he fought in Iraq; it was one of those 'hometown hero' articles."

My hands were shaking as I smoked. I could almost feel the final straw being placed upon my back. If the world thought *he* was a hero, then life truly was fucking pointless.

"Michael—"

"Michael—"

"Michael … what are you doing?" she asked.

She was looking down at my hand. I followed her eyes. My right hand was holding my cigarette, but my left was dialing a phone number. I put the phone to my ear.

"Hey, Wilson," I said.

"What's up?"

"You've got to hear this." I relayed what Natalie had just told me about the article. It wasn't much, but Wilson didn't care. "Let's burn his fucking house down," he said. And never before had I been so sure of the intentionality of six words. *Let's burn his fucking house down*. Wilson meant it.

"Colonel Lollydash was no fucking hero. He was a disgrace to the fucking uniform. The thought that anyone…" I could hear the strain in his voice coming through the phone. I could practically feel the heat from his anger. "There are real fucking heroes—"

"I know—"

"But not him—"

"I know, man—"

"*Anyone* but him—"

"I know—"

"They should've kicked the bastard out."

Phil Collins's "In the Air Tonight" was the theme song one soldier had given Colonel Lollydash in Iraq. The song was about letting an awful human being drown, rather than saving him. And it perfectly reflected how we all felt about Colonel Lollydash. We would've happily watched him drown.

He was the epitome of the false soldier. The dereliction of duty. The lies. The cowardice. Now, however, it seemed as though the joke was on us. The world thought Lollydash was a hero, and there was nothing funny about that.

"I can't even … how this is even…" Wilson was stammering.

I lit another cigarette. I could hear Wilson doing the same.

Wilson continued stammering. "How … why …" and it was a few seconds before he actually said something coherent. "Someone needs to write down the shit that really happened."

"I know, man."

"You should write that shit down."

"And say what?"

"The fucking truth, man. Talk about how shitty things were. Call the heroes, heroes, and call the shitbirds, shitbirds."

"I don't know—"

"I'm serious—you should do it. You kept journals in Iraq. Write that shit down."

"No—"

He directed some of his anger toward me. "Fuck, man. Just

fuckin' do it. Who the fuck else will? Lollydash probably won't be the only asshole to be called a hero who shouldn't."

The car jerked to a stop. I hadn't noticed that Natalie had pulled back on the road and started driving again. We were in front of her house, she idled the engine. She took off her seatbelt, and looked over at me. "Are you all right to drive?" she mouthed quietly.

I cupped my hand over the cellphone speaker. "Yeah, yeah. Totally sober now."

"Okay. I'll see you tomorrow? Or sometime this week?"

"Yeah, yeah. Sure."

Natalie got out of the car and I slid over to the driver's seat. I shut the door. "So what do we do now?" I asked Wilson.

"I already told you, man," Wilson was saying. "We burn his fucking house down."

I put the car in drive.

24

I was standing in the lobby of a hotel just outside of Boston. It was pouring, and the trees were shaking. As the automatic doors slid open, an elderly couple walked in. We could feel the wind. Zeke, who was just about to sell me some Ambien, stopped. "Let's do this outside," he said. "Fewer people around." He put on his hood and walked toward the same automatic doors. Just outside the hotel, underneath a black-and-white awning, he smoked a cigarette and leaned against the wall.

The night after Natalie told me about the Lollydash article, I did all I could to put it out of mind. But I learned then that it wasn't the sort of memory that could fade with drugs and alcohol. I couldn't shake it. Being over there had touched something fundamental in my being. Lollydash, and other bullshit lackeys like him, had ignited something in me that I couldn't change. A moral injury that wouldn't heal. The wrong people being called heroes. It tears at you more than you'd imagine. Makes you doubt whether or not you ever knew what a real hero was. Maybe you had it wrong. Maybe they were right. Maybe anything.

"You watch the Bruins game last night?" Zeke asked.

Zeke worked at the hotel and was on break, overnight security or something. He pulled his sweater tight around his body. The rain was blowing sideways, and the awning offered little to no protection. I had no idea what game was on last night. "No, man. Must have missed that one."

"Well it was a fucking good one." He continued rambling about sports, despite the fact that I knew next to nothing about them, and couldn't care less.

My feet were becoming more and more soaked the longer he talked. He mentioned something about Claude Julie, the coach of the Bruins, but my thoughts flitted toward Natalie. I hadn't talked to her in three days; this time, I hoped she'd gotten the message.

Zeke was talking so fast that he made me feel as though I were drunk, which I wished I was. "It was incredible. You should've seen the way the puck…"

The rain hit my face, and I remembered how the rain in Iraq was different. It was thinner than in Massachusetts, more spread out, and somehow sharper. My cigarette went out in the downpour. I lit another, which Zeke took to mean that I was enjoying listening to him, and that I intended to stay longer.

"After we finish, you can come inside if you want and hang out." He jerked his thumb toward the hotel. "I've got a TV at my station." That was the problem with guys like Zeke; everyone was always coming and going. They bought their stuff from him and left. Drug dealers were some of the loneliest people in the world.

I took a drag. "Yeah, sure, what the hell," I told him. "I could hang out for a little while."

A few minutes later, we were settled into his security station. It was a small room, hidden off in a secluded part of the hotel: two dusty, uncomfortable-looking chairs, a small table with two TV monitors on top. They were playing the different hotel cameras on a loop. We could hear the falling swish of rain tapping against the ground and building. Zeke leaned back in the chair farthest from the door. I sat in the other. He then rose to his feet, grabbed two beers from a small refrigerator under the table, and found a late-night talk show: David Letterman was in the middle of his monologue. Zeke cracked open his beer. "Watch this," he said, putting his beer down. He picked up a large flashlight that was sitting on a table next to the security TV. He spun it around in his hand, like an old cowboy with a revolver. After a few rotations, he smiled. "Pretty cool, huh?"

My willpower was strained. "Yeah, man. Pretty cool."

Within minutes, we were talking about the military. Zeke had a million questions, and he asked them all in that rapid-fire way of his. "How was it over there?" "Kill anyone?" "See anyone die?" "Did you almost die?" "Girls must love a man in uniform, right?" "What did you do over there?" At least Zeke had an innocence about him, almost as though he were a child asking his big brother about the war. It wasn't until he had asked about a dozen, though, that I started to pay attention. "Did you find God over there?"

I hadn't ever been asked that question before. I asked why he wanted to know.

"I don't know. I've just heard people say something like that. They go to war and find God or something."

I picked up his flashlight, spun it around in my hand. I laughed to myself for a moment: of all places, of all nights, to be proselytized to by a drug dealer. We chugged our beers, and then Zeke grabbed two more.

"So did you?" he asked as we each popped a Vicodin along with our new beers.

I sipped, unsure of what to say. "Yeah… I don't know, man. I guess… maybe. Or maybe I lost him."

Zeke kicked his feet up on the table next to the TV, next to David Letterman's head and desk. "Yeah. I hear you," he said. "I once thought about going to seminary school, becoming a priest but… things happen. Like one time—"

In war, everyone had their moments with God. Those moments when we'd yell, scream, and swear at God: "Just give me one more chance. I promise, things will be different." Every person who'd ever been to war knew those prayers. The bombs flying, bodies falling, trouble brewing at home. "There are no atheists in foxholes," we'd say, because even the most nihilistic among us, when faced with the reality of war, was forced to give in. "God help me."

"I got news for you—Colonel Lollydash did not save the president of the United States."

"What's that?" Zeke asked.

All I could think about was Colonel Lollydash. The lies he must've told to receive his Bronze Star for *heroism*. "Three grenades jumped on." "Lifting two Chinook helicopters off the ground with one finger while holding off a thousand enemy troops." Several friends and I had refused to receive all the awards we were nominated for. We told our commanders, "We're not here for the metal."

"You all right, man?"

But our commanders didn't listen. In the end, we were forced to stand up there and receive our awards—ordered, actually. We had no choice. Awards made *them* look good!

"My mother wanted me to be a priest," Zeke explained. "She always wanted a priest in the family, to take care of her when she got older—"

"You get asked to lie, man, over there ... about mortar attacks and some shit, so this other guy, somebody, can receive a Combat Action Badge. 'Course, I never would do it, so I get the silent treatment. I become the fucking enemy. 'Never trust a man with a chest full of metal,' that's what Denti and I say, 'Unless the metal is shrapnel.'"

"Makes sense, right?"

"The fucking problem though is that guys who don't give a shit about awards don't get promoted... But the guys who care about awards—and I mean care enough to lie about them—they get promoted because they have all the hardware. Meanwhile, the good soldiers get out because they see all these shitbirds getting promoted—"

Zeke asked if I wanted another beer.

"Thanks."

"That's some intense shit you're talking about, man."

"It all seems so fucking pointless," I told Zeke.

"The war?" he asked.

"Yeah, that and everything else."

What the army failed to tell us was that there was no glory—that there *is* no glory—after the war. Parades? That wasn't glory. Saving a life, surviving a bombing, working forty-eight hours straight, no break, no food. Pushing yourself for something greater than yourself—that was glory. There was nothing left after combat. The only ones who keep their glory are the dead, and now that I was back, I was only a taker. I am only a taker.

"I've got to go," I told him.

Before I knew it, I was back in my bedroom, sitting at a desk covered with a half-dozen books, paper, pens, a carton of cigarettes, a dozen empty beer cans, a dozen full beer cans, and a bottle of Ambien from Zeke. My heart thudded in my chest. I had decided that Ambien was how I wanted it to end. It seemed the easiest way. No mess to clean up, no trigger to pull, no pain. During our pre-deployment training, one soldier had tried to kill himself using pills, just like Gunner. And just like Gunner, he was found passed out in the bathroom. This soldier had taken the pills, not because he was depressed, but because he was afraid of going to war, which made suicide make even less sense. But suicide often makes no sense. Before his attempted suicide, he had tried to get out of the deployment by getting a swastika tattooed on his arm. The tattoo didn't get him out of the deployment, but the suicide did.

The thing I was most worried about was my threshold. I had taken so many Ambien in the past that I had no idea how much would be enough. I'd already taken one with Zeke, and another since I'd been home. I estimated I had another twenty to go. I picked up the closest book, put it down, and picked up my cigarettes instead. I lit one and then rested my feet up on the desk. Smoking and drinking, I could feel the thoughts from the war pulsing. Twenty more pills. Then everything would be done, gone. One down, nineteen to go.

On top of my desk, a copy of Shakespeare's *Henry V*. I picked up the play, another pill. Eighteen to go.

The ending of *Henry V* tells the story of King Henry and the battle of Agincourt. It's a pivotal battle, and King Henry is uncertain if his men will stay and fight. They'd just endured several smaller battles, followed by a two-hundred-and-fifty-mile march; they're tired and hungry, and the French outnumber them ten to one. It's the classic underdog story.

The night before the battle, King Henry walks around his camp, wracking his brain, his heart, the depth of his being, wondering whether or not his men are ready, willing, and able to fight. He consults with his generals, and he talks with his troops—in disguise, of course. To fight or not to fight? It was what Saint John of the Cross described in his poem the *Dark Night of the Soul*. A man lies in spiritual crisis, with a great decision before him. Two paths to choose. But which one? Finally, King Henry gives a speech, a speech in which he allows any man who wants to return home to do so without penalty. For according to King Henry, any man who would return home does not deserve to join their ranks: "The fewer men, the greater share of honor." He goes on:

> *… From this day to the ending of the world,*
> *but we in it shall be remembered-*
> *we few, we happy few, we band of brothers;*
> *for he to-day that sheds his blood with me*
> *shall be my brother…*

King Henry and his men fought bravely in the Battle of Agincourt, and despite the odds, they defeated the French and returned home heroes.

From the play, though, it was easy to tell that Shakespeare had never fought in a real war. Because if he had, he would've known that the dark night of the soul comes *after* the battle, not before. Joining the military was the easiest decision I have ever made; going to war was the second easiest. Coming home was the hard part.

Hundreds of years of history, hundreds of years of battles, hundreds of years of warriors fighting, killing, and dying.

The reality of what I was doing was hitting me. Only seventeen more to go.

This was it, I thought, and dumped more into my hand. I breathed deeply and looked at the pills. Just do it. No. Don't. Do it. Don't. I couldn't breathe as I thought. My family. Friends. The end. I was trying hard to breathe, to focus, to make sense, to make a decision. It was one of those moments where you realize you don't control your body as much as you think you do. My eyes went to the pen and paper next to the pills.

The cap of the bottle lay on my desk, a half dozen pills in my sweaty hand. I thought of Wilson's words. "Who else would do it?" Who would tell Crade's story? Who would tell the truth about Lollydash? I thought of all the bullshit I'd heard and seen since coming home. People had no idea what really happened in war—or didn't care. I put the pills down and took out the journal I'd kept in Iraq. I placed it next to a blank sheet of paper on the desk. The thoughts, feelings, and flashbacks—I wanted it all to end. I looked at the pills that I had placed on top of *Henry V.* But the thought of leaving an unfinished book, the one inside me—a man can't kill himself with an unfinished book. I took a deep breath; it came easier this time. I closed my eyes and put myself back in Iraq. I began writing as though still there:

Week 1, Day 1, Mosul, Iraq
0900 Hours, Airfield
[My first day in Iraq...]

Loaded with gear—a three-pound helmet, thirty-pound armored vest, eight-pound weapon, and thirty-pound rucksack—we're running. There are four hundred of us from thirty-seven different states across the United States. All of us have been

brought together to run the 178th Combat Support
Hospital. In the plane, we were briefed about how
the bad guys love to bomb the airfield even though
we're in Kurd territory, supposedly our allies....

The sky is yellow, orange, and brown scratched
together—not like the blue sky back in Boston.
An Iraqi man is staring at us; I see him. He wears a
black-and-white turban, which I know means he's
been to Mecca. I'm not sure if I've seen skin tone
like his before; it's golden auburn. I notice that it's
the same color as the buildings, and the buildings
are the same color as the sand blowing in my face.
They're the same color as the sky. I think that if I
were fifty feet away and there was a pile of sand, a
building, and a naked Iraqi man, I wouldn't be able
to differentiate between them. They all look like they
belong together: the tiny buildings, the man with a
face that's tired, the sand, the sky, and the sun.

In the distance is a dome, clearly American
made; it doesn't belong at all. We're not supposed
to be here either? It's the northern part of the
country, a hot spot in Iraq.

I paused after writing my first entry, lit another cigarette. I was
starting to feel good, hopeful, like things might be all right. But
my stomach was also starting to bother me. I felt like I needed to
throw up—

25

Almost exactly one year later, I woke up in bed. I tore the sheets off. My pajamas were soaking wet. Did I just piss myself? How much did I drink last night? Had I been drinking?

I reached down, touched my pajamas, and then brought my fingers toward my nose. I sniffed.

My new girlfriend, Laura, stirred on her part of the bed.

Did I just have a fucking wet dream?

She leaned over, eyes still closed. "What's up Sweetie? Everything okay?" Laura was this spunky hippie type I had met through a friend of a friend. She had short brown hair, a killer smile, and this annoying habit of always calling me "Sweetie."

I pitched my legs over the bed. "I was… just getting up to go the bathroom."

She rolled over, already asleep again.

I speed walked to the laundry room, and tore off my pajamas. A wet dream? I hadn't had one since high school, more than ten years ago. I threw my pajamas into the dirty clothes pile, picked up a pair of dirty shorts from the day before, and crawled back into bed. I lay there, wracking my brain, vaguely remembering that I'd been dreaming about Jennifer Aniston; maybe Courtney Cox was there, too. Whoever it was, I definitely had sex with her.

Unable to drift back to sleep, I thought about the previous twelve hours.

"A lot of people get nervous and cancel," the psychologist had said as I took a seat in her office. "I'm glad you decided to come." That should have been my first warning. "So, tell me. What brought you here today?"

Even after having been in therapy, I still didn't feel comfortable talking about myself. "Nothing."

She looked unconvinced. "Nothing brought you here today?"

"Well, I guess I'm feeling a little anxious, like I want to start drinking and smoking and doing drugs again."

"And you used to do all those things?"

"Yeah."

"Any stresses in your life?"

I leaned back in the chair. I told her how one year earlier, I had been in my room, slowly working my way through a bottle of Ambien. I told her how things changed that night, how I started writing, how I started thinking of Colonel Lollydash reading a real account of our deployment, written by me. I talked about Laura, too, and how much I cared about her—and how scared I was of screwing things up, like I had with Natalie. But mostly, I talked about my time in the army, lingering feelings about what I'd seen and gone through. I told her about people I'd seen die, the times I almost died, the friends from the war who were struggling. Crade, my good friend from Iraq, who had attempted to kill himself twice over there—and received no help from our commanders.

"Interesting. Interesting," she said, in that vague psychologist tone that always pissed me off. And then, after everything I told her. What did she want to talk about?

Natalie and Laura.

She wanted to know more about them. How I had gone from being a "nerd in high school" to a self-proclaimed lothario. And why I was so afraid of losing Laura.

I thought for a moment, "Well… have you ever heard of something called the Boston Lair?"

She shook her head, and I started with a story about David and his dating class, and then carried it to Gunner and Natalie and then to Laura.

"Writing just gave me that passion. You know? Focusing on something bigger than myself… Laura's the same way. She makes me a better person…"

"Interesting. Interesting," she said again. "I think I can definitely help you… how about we hook you up?" She motioned to a computer to my right.

I nodded.

She asked if it was all right to put the device on my head.

I nodded.

She asked again if it was all right to put the device on my head. I nodded.

She put a swimming-cap device on my head and started pushing a blueish goo through holes in the cap.

"To get a reading of your brain," she said as she pushed more and more through the holes.

The texture felt like a mixture of Vaseline and KY Jelly, and it smelled just the same. Once she was done, my head felt like a bucket of Jell-O, and I smelled like the back of a strip club—and not the section for high rollers, either; this was strictly meth-head smell.

Twenty minutes later, after she had hooked up electrodes to the Jell-O bucket and scanned my brain, she told me it was time to start the next phase.

Neurofeedback. I still couldn't believe I'd agreed to it. "Let us rewire your brain," the online ad had said. It promised to help fight addiction, ADD, ADHD, memory problems, and even PTSD.

What the hell was I thinking?

"Free for Veterans." That's what I was thinking. This new therapeutic process was somehow supposed to rewire the neurons in my brain. Make me happier, more focused, a better person. I knew I needed to get rid of certain feelings, once and for all. My craving for a drink, smoke, or Vicodin. I was building a new life for myself with Laura. I was willing to try anything. And I never could turn away a good deal. Nothing beats free.

My legs shook. "Relax," she told me. "It's painless and actually kind of fun. There might be some interesting side effects, though..."

She then hooked up an '80s-style rubber headband with electrodes built into it. As the computer screen popped up, we were staring at a racecar that looked like it belonged in a video game.

"You'll control the car with you brain," she said. "Every time your brain does something good, the car will go faster and your brain will get a reward, like a sound or image. Every time your brain does something bad, your car will go slower and your brain will not get a reward. Got it?"

I nodded.

She pressed play, and my car started moving. I tried to will it forward, faster, but it didn't work. I got distracted. The car didn't move. I took a deep breath, tried to clear my mind, as she had advised. The car started to move. The car stopped. Fuck. Move, you fucking car, MOVE! I breathed. Calmed down. The car started. It went fast. I started beating the other cars. My car slowed down. Stopped. FUCK THIS! This is pointless. Stupid. I breathed. Calmed down. The car started. It went fast. I passed the other cars.

"We're done for today," she said. Thirty minutes had somehow passed. It had only felt like two. The doctor took the swimming cap off, the goo dripping down my neck. "Make sure you shower thoroughly when you get home," she said, as though maybe I'd forget to wash off the pound of Vaseline and KY Jelly.

The second I walked out of her office, I began to feel like I'd downed a dozen cups of coffee and had smoked a carton of cigarettes—not in a good way, either. Laura called as I started the car.

"How'd it go?" she asked. I hung up as she was still talking. I was agitated. I'd never hung up on her before. I felt angry. I tried to process what had happened, but my mind was racing.

Later that night, Laura came over and I apologized for hanging up on her earlier. She wasn't fine with just an apology, though, and instead of brushing over things like Natalie would, she insisted on talking. My mind was still in a foggy state, but had calmed down enough. So we talked. About everything. Her. Me. *Us.* I even told her about David's dating classes—leaving out some of the 'techniques' or 'tricks' that might still be evident in my behavior—an embarrassing fact I'd been dreading admitting. She was fine with it though—accepted it, laughed with me about it. It was a conversation I wouldn't have been able to laugh about like that a year earlier. And after we had said everything that we had to say (maybe even a little bit more than that), we relaxed on the couch and watched a rerun of *Friends.*

When I woke up nine hours later, I walked to the bathroom to take my morning piss. I heard Laura in the laundry room, doing a load of wash.

"Oh my God. What is this?" she yelled.

Fuck. It wasn't all just a dream.

She held my pajama pants stretched out in front of her, like something toxic. My stain was right there in the middle.

I was fifteen all over again. Only this time, instead of my mother asking me why I'd suddenly decided to start doing my own laundry, my girlfriend was asking the questions. My panic was unnecessary, though. When she saw my face, she laughed, and let it drop.

Later that evening, I called a different neurofeedback psychologist—one who was twenty minutes closer. I told her that I'd already had my first session the day before.

"Any interesting side effects?" she asked.

Did she know? I wondered. No, she couldn't know.

"...you mean, like dreams?"

"Sure. Could be anything."

"I guess I had an interesting night—"

"Nightmares?"

Cue nostalgic look upward, and reminiscence of sex with Jennifer Aniston. "No, definitely not nightmares."

She went on to explain that the brain was a powerful organ, and that if it could wire itself for nightmares, then it could certainly rewire itself for something else, something less depressing.

"Typically, we like to start off with a trial run to see how things go. How does a three-month trial sound?"

I smiled. "Three months..." I paused. It seemed as good a timeframe as any other. "Okay... three months it is."

EPILOGUE

Real-life endings are never what you expect, because those magical moments that catch us off guard can never be predicted. When I first got back from Iraq, I never would've imagined that it would be writing—something I'd been doing for years—that would bring me out of my funk. But it was the perfect distraction. The perfect mission: write a true war story!

And that's exactly what I did. Two years after that night in my bedroom, a memoir about my deployment to Iraq was traditionally published: *Mass Casualties: A Young Medic's True Story of Death, Deception and Dishonor in Iraq* (Adams Media). I was twenty-three at the time, and in the years since, I've received thousands of e-mails from veterans and their spouses (either with similar stories to tell, or inquiring about advice for dealing with PTSD). It was after reading and responding to all those e-mails that I decided to publish this memoir.

Nothing happened overnight, but it only took that one night for things to begin to change. After a short struggle, I stopped drinking. I stopped taking Vicodin and Ambien, and I quit smoking. Then I quit smoking again, and then I stopped smoking three more times.

So why these stories, instead of the thousand others that happened during this same time period? Simple, really. These are the ones that stick out. Even though they're kind of silly, and all that really happened was I got in a few fights, got drunk, got laid, and was a bit depressed. But some things just leave an impression, and as in all aspects of life, you never know what you're going to remember, or what's going to have the biggest impact. I've only been to Iraq once, but I've stepped off that plane a thousand times. I've felt that sun beating down on my neck a thousand times. I remember sitting on the roof of the hospital, chain-smoking cigarettes and playing the guitar. I remember playing baseball inside the hospital, and the feeling of holding a broom handle as a bat as I swung hard at an ACE-bandage baseball. I remember what I was eating when I heard that Crade tried to kill himself. And I remember the feeling of fascination as I watched a unit of misfits, from thirty-seven different states, somehow come together to run a hospital that would save thousands of lives. That's what our memories are for, though: reliving and remembering, again, and again, and again. Whether we like it or not.

Sometimes a soldier returns home and all he can do is share his story in the hopes that somehow, in some way, it helps another soldier make sense of things. And although the stories may not be perfect, sometimes just sharing is enough to make a difference.

Here are the brutal facts. Since returning home, out of the roughly two hundred people who served in my hospital in Iraq, three soldiers have killed themselves—including my good friend Crade. A handful of the other soldiers have gone through drug-rehabilitation clinics; over a dozen more have been treated at PTSD clinics, with several qualifying for disability. Gunner, last I heard, is alive and doing well, having begun therapy. Wolfenstein and Commando, I can only imagine, are still lurking out there, whispering to each other in the corners of Boston bars. Natalie, Samantha, and Wilson are also doing well. As for Colonel Lollydash... well, he's still in the army and has risen in rank, of course. He's also still calling himself a hero and being praised as one, while so many real heroes—guys like Gunner, Wilson, and so many others—struggle every day in the United States, unnoticed, unappreciated, and unaided.